NARC

NARC

THE ADVENTURES OF A FEDERAL AGENT

by Melvin L. Hanks

HASTINGS HOUSE • PUBLISHERS

NEW YORK

B
H 2413 h

Library of Congress Cataloging in Publication Data

Hanks, Melvin L
Narc: the adventures of a Federal agent.

1. Narcotics, Control of—United States.
2. Police—Correspondence, reminiscences, etc.
I. Title
HV5825.H22   363.2'092'4 [B]   72-13711
ISBN 0-8038-5025-5

PUBLISHED SIMULTANEOUSLY IN CANADA BY
SAUNDERS OF TORONTO, LTD., DON MILLS, ONTARIO

PRINTED IN THE UNITED STATES OF AMERICA

Contents

Chapter	Page
Foreword	7
The *Marbella*	11
The Mexican Border	34
The Chin Shieu Case	44
The Jade Tong Ring	63
A Female Racketeer	91
A Hijacking Swim	96
The Rum Runners	102
A Creature From The Deep	113
Border Gold	117
Spies and Smugglers	125
Some Interesting Characters	145
Strayed Contraband	155
An Oriental Diplomat	162
A Lazy Third Mate	167
Japanese Sampans	170
Paneled Walls	175
Suicide Preferred	178
Recollections	183

Foreword

Narcotics were sold at public auction by United States marshals on post office steps before 1912.

Drugs seized by the government for non-payment of import duties were disposed of in this manner.

Prior to 1912, no laws in the United States prohibited the sale and use of addictive drugs.

Due to the increasing problem of addiction, the Narcotic Export and Import Act, passed in 1912, prohibited the importation of raw opium, opium prepared for smoking, and the derivatives of opium—heroin and morphine. This act also prohibited the importation of cocaine. The only exceptions made were for sufficient quantities of these drugs to provide for the medicinal needs of the nation, and these importations were under the strict supervision of the government.

Until recent times, marijuana was not on the list of contraband drugs. In the last few years, however, marijuana and several lesser known drugs considered to be dangerous have been added to the prohibited list.

In my opinion the narcotics situation in the United States today is most alarming and considerably worse than ever before.

Since Castro gained control, Cuba not only trains American revolutionaries but, supplied and backed by Red China, is deluging our nation with addictive drugs. Cuba sends spies and agents experienced in narcotics activities to take up residence in all parts of the United States.

The current special attention and intensified efforts of the governments of Mexico and the United States to stop narcotic smuggling have brought into sharper focus a long-existing problem: The common border of 1522 miles has always been a source of difficulty.

In the early 1930s, a cooperative effort was also arranged to prevent narcotic smuggling from Mexico into the United States. We found the smuggling across the Mexican border different from elsewhere, usually consisting of small unconnected groups, or even individual operations. The Customs Bureau had been faced with well-organized and heavily-financed smuggling groups from Europe and the Orient, in contrast to Mexican smuggling.

We cooperated closely. Mexican authorities escorted some of us American enforcement officers into remote areas and assisted in destroying the opium crop. Mexico, however, is a large country, so that the crops we found and destroyed were only a small percentage of the total.

Due to the many isolated Mexican farmers who depend on an opium crop for a livelihood, and also because of administrative problems, preventing smuggling across the border is difficult and complicated.

My assignment by the U.S. Customs to specialize in preventing or apprehending smuggled narcotic drugs spanned many years. My district covered the Mexican border from El Paso, Texas to the Pacific, and the entire Pacific coast to the Canadian line. It also included the Hawaiian Islands, with occasional investigations in China and Japan.

We Customs Agents found ourselves fully involved. It

was a matter of continuous, cooperative effort to try to prevent smuggling or apprehend smuggled goods and the smugglers. There was no time to relax and celebrate the winning of a particular case. Family life and personal relationships necessarily were subordinated to our work. At times we were forced to stake out and maintain continuous surveillance of a suspect for long hours, day and night. Meals and social schedules often were neglected, and sleep not to be counted on.

Most of the contraband narcotics arriving in Hawaii and Pacific coast ports originated in the southern provinces of China or Indo-China, and in some notable instances in Japan.

One of our trouble spots was Puget Sound. A large number of British ships with Chinese crews were on regular runs between China, Japan and Canadian and U. S. ports in Puget Sound.

We were fortunate in being able to work closely with the Royal Canadian Mounted Police, a well-trained and efficient organization. Sergeant John Healy of that service specialized, at that time, in narcotic smuggling. Together, we had considerable success.

Narcotics smuggling from China directly to the Pacific coast had been largely cut down due to lack of trade between China and the United States and Canada. However, Canada's diplomatic recognition of Red China and the reopening of trade relations by the U.S. could impose a mammoth burden on the United States and Canadian Customs. Chinese narcotics smugglers can be expected to begin again their dope smuggling directly to the North American continent.

Our Atlantic coast must contend with drugs grown principally in Turkey and other Middle Eastern countries. Much of this is processed and manufactured in Marseilles,

France. Cocaine originating in South America gives Customs officers an additional burden.

The Oriental smugglers, particularly the Chinese, were and probably still are, the cleverest and most difficult to apprehend. One reason for this situation is the method of hiring Chinese crews for vessels calling at U. S. ports. A compradore or boss of a seaman's hiring hall in China knows that he must hire for any one ship only those who are members of one particular Chinese family Tong. All Chinese crewmen must be members of the same Tong, otherwise considerable trouble results. No Tong member would dream of informing the U. S. Customs or anyone else about any contraband on his ship, even though a large reward might be offered. He fully understands that his life expectation would be nil if he should betray his clannish family Tong.

All nations or civilized communities from earliest times have imposed duties on merchandise entering their domain. They have also prohibited certain goods from entry.

Long ago Spain demanded fees from all vessels entering or leaving the Mediterranean. These fees were paid at the small seaport of Tarifa. This accounts for our modern use of the word "tariff".

At the time this nation was founded and extending well into the present century, the Customs officers enforced most of the Federal laws, including those now enforced by the Bureau of Internal Revenue, the Immigration Service, the Narcotics Bureau and the Departments of Justice and Commerce, as well as others. However, the duty of preventing violation of the Tariff Act and apprehending smugglers has remained with the Customs Bureau.

The Marbella

RUMORS—WHISPERS—TIPS!

They are at once the bane and boon of a Customs Agent's life. Ninety-nine times out of a hundred the rumor is false, the whisper malicious, the tip fabricated. But the hundredth time may pay off in sudden and dramatic fashion.

In San Francisco, in 1931, I heard the first in a series of rumors that led to the opening of what came to be known, in Customs circles, as "The *Marbella* Case".

At that time I was Customs Agent-at-Large on the Pacific coast, under supervision of Thomas J. Gorman, Deputy Commissioner of Customs in Washington, D.C.

The rumor about a combine for smuggling opium by the boatload came to us through a "stool pigeon".

"The boats will be handled by rum runners," said the informer, "and the dough's coming from a tong. They'll put the cargo aboard in Hong Kong and peddle it in the U.S. There's a couple of cons running the deal and plenty of cash behind them."

He was a ratty little fellow, Eurasian by birth and Skid Row by choice. I did not put too much credence in his report, especially since he was an addict himself. Most drug

11

users have pipe dreams of the day when narcotics will be as plentiful and cheap as tobacco.

But I heard the story again in Portland and then once more in Seattle. Each time more fanciful details were added. It was embellished with pirate ships and Chinese junks, sailing across the Pacific laden with millions of dollars worth of opium and aliens.

Some of the basic information, however, remained curiously the same in each telling.

A wealthy Chinese and a big-time rum runner, both serving sentences in a penitentiary, were the brains behind the venture. The boat was to be manned by rum runners and gangsters, but a tong would be responsible for securing the cargo in China and peddling it when it arrived in the United States.

When I began to consider the enormous proportions such an operation could develop, it seemed to justify investigation.

Opium at the time was selling in the United States for twenty-five dollars an ounce, wholesale. (Today it is many times that.) There are six and two-thirds ounces in the standard opium five-tael container. The drug is retailed by peddlers in bindles of about seven grains—bringing the retail value of a tin to around six hundred dollars. These same tins could be bought in Macao, the opium-processing center of the Orient, for around five to seven dollars.

At the same time, aliens were bringing a thousand dollars a head, with part of the money paid in advance and the remainder collected as soon as they landed on American soil. There was no chance of the alien welshing on his debt, either. Upon arrival, he was put into bondage until the money was paid. Should the cash not be forthcoming, it would take only an anonymous phone call to the Immigration Service to finish his American sojourn. Deported, the alien would meet death at the hands of those he bilked—and he well knew it.

A shipload of opium at more than $150 a tin profit, wholesale, (and each tin takes up less cargo space than a can of tobacco) and $1,000 for each alien aboard could make an immense profit for its owner in a single successful trip!

When I was in San Francisco again, I sought out another informer, a white man who, as a long-time opium addict, was accepted by the inner circle of tongs.

"What do you know about this big company that's being formed to bring opium across on its own boats?" I asked him.

He scratched his head, shedding a white shower of dandruff over his coat collar, and promised to find out.

A week later he called me and asked me to meet him at a small Chinatown cafe. He could hardly wait to get into a booth and pull the curtains before whispering, "It's on the level. They bringing it over by the boatload, starting next month!"

I demanded details.

"Don't know any," he said. "I wouldn't open my trap at all if I didn't owe you something. The only thing I hear now is that the birds behind it are in McNeil pen. One of them is a Chink who used to be a big shot around this town."

"But how do you know it's on the level?"

Again he scratched dandruff from his hair and then looked at me triumphantly. "Because the Chinks are getting ready to put out the dough for the first load. They got to pay half of their first orders in advance."

The rumors were becoming more credible. If the local Chinese were ready to pay, it looked as if the scheme was finally going into effect.

So I went to Tacoma and then by boat to the federal penitentiary at McNeil Island.

The rumor was unknown to the prison heads. But when I went over the register of inmates, I found two names that seemed to back up the stories I had heard.

Wong Tai, biggest opium smuggler the Customs Service had ever put behind bars, up until that time, and Eugene Kohler, notorious West Coast rum runner, were in the same cell block.

At that instant I believed the rumor to be a fact. If there were two men in the world who could provide the daring and the financial backing for such a gigantic smuggling scheme, Gene Kohler and Wong Tai were those men. Consider their backgrounds:

First, the infamous Wong Tai—chubby and blandly angelic of face—had a long history of eluding justice before he was convicted. As a matter of fact, he had been born into the business of smuggling. His uncle, Wong Quai Sun, had been king of the opium smugglers in his day and, in the course of his activities, had brought about the bankruptcy of the great China Mail Steamship Line almost single handed.

In an effort to stem the flow of opium being smuggled by Wong's combine, Customs Agents searched every Oriental vessel that entered the harbors. The China Mail Line, although its owners were innocent of smuggling, found it impossible to continue to pay the fines on the opium brought over on their ships. At last, they went into bankruptcy.

After years of work, the Customs Bureau finally managed to collect evidence that convicted Wong Quai Sun. He was deported to his native China.

Wong merely turned over the machinery of his organization to his American-educated nephew, Wong Tai. Eventually, Wong Tai was caught, convicted and sent to McNeil Island.

The warden told me he would be released in a few weeks. Though he was due for deportation, he still could direct his operations from China.

As for Kohler, even his enemies conceded he had been top bootlegger until the Moss Beach Landing affair. He had started early in Prohibition days, smuggling liquor from British Columbia into Washington. But as his business increased he changed from small shipments by automobile to big shipments by boat, transferring headquarters and operations to California, Oregon and Washington coasts. He used a "mother" ship to bring the big loads down the coast. Since he had once been a fishboat captain, he knew all the bays and inlets of the Pacific coast. Thus he was able to change his base of operations to avoid patrols.

Kohler feared the law less than he did hijackers. In the summer of 1925, hijacking was big business. Kohler was using the Moss Beach Landing, just south of San Francisco, as the place for unloading his current shipments when he received a tip that hijackers were on his trail.

He purchased a small arsenal of machine guns.

"They can have it—if they can get it!" he told his crew.

He posted the best shots among them on the surrounding hills.

The bootlegger's informant, however, had been wrong. It was not hijackers, but a group of government agents and deputy sheriffs who hid behind the dunes under the cover of darkness that night in July.

At 1 a.m. there was the muffled roar of high-powered engines. The speedboats left the ship, heavily loaded. Minutes later they stopped their engines and drifted on to the beach, lights out.

As the boats grounded, the officers ran out from behind the dunes, unaware that Kohler's men were posted on the hills above them. There was a rattle of machine gun fire as the men on the hills opened up. The rum runners in the boats leaped out, using the hulls as barricades. Agents and deputies were caught in a deadly trap between two firing lines.

At last, Kohler recognized his opponents and ordered

the men on shore to "Hold fire," but his voice did not reach the gunmen on the hills. Again they fired, and though they fled a moment later, a deputy sheriff lay dead in the sand and three agents, badly wounded, watched Kohler and his men in the boats surrender to the officers who were left.

That was how Gene Kohler happened to be in McNeil Island penitentiary with Wong Tai—and why I decided to stand by and see what happened when these two men were released.

In a few weeks, the big doors of the prison swung open to let Wong Tai step out—a free man for a brief moment. As he walked across the boundary separating the Federal property from that of the state of Washington, an Immigration Inspector closed in on each side.

They placed Wong Tai in custody for deportation and took him to the detention building in Seattle.

I contacted the Immigration officials.

"Keep a check of every visitor who comes to see Wong Tai while he's in your custody," I requested.

They agreed to do me this favor.

The list they gave me later for the three week period before Wong Tai's hearing was completed and he boarded a ship to return to China contained forty-six names!

Most of them were wealthy Chinese brokers and merchants from San Francisco. Some, however, had traveled to Seattle from New York, and though they apparently came only to bid him farewell, I felt certain they were establishing business contacts at the same time. The compiling of facts on these visitors was the start of our files on the *Marbella* case. Before it was closed those files were voluminous.

With Wong Tai off for China, my attention turned to Kohler. He was released three weeks later and went to San Francisco. When our men turned in their reports on his movements I discovered that he had spent his time visiting many of the men who had said goodbye to Wong Tai earlier.

He also was seen on the waterfront day after day—looking at schooners.

"He's looking for a ship around a hundred feet in length", my men told me. "Says he's interested in a South Sea expedition!"

Apparently San Francisco had no boat that suited him. Kohler moved on down to San Pedro, the harbor for Los Angeles. Again he looked over many boats for sale.

And now a new character entered our surveillance. Kohler met a man named Sigmund Ypma.

Ypma was an old Dutch sea captain. At the time he was "on the beach without a berth", but he had skippered a number of small freighters and had, at one time, been master of a South Sea islands tramp ship.

Apparently Kohler and Ypma came to an agreement. Kohler returned to San Francisco but soon afterward wired the old captain thirty dollars with instructions to join him there. When we picked up their trail, they had added still another person to their partnership—a dark, slightly-built young man of Spanish or Mexican origin who was using the name of George Rumbler. The three went to Seattle, then to Vancouver, B. C. Several days later I learned from agents there that they had bought a schooner, 136 feet long.

Ypma was listed as owner. Obviously this would make him the loser in case of any misadventure.

The *Hedwig* was an auxiliary sailing rig. The motors would be useful in navigating the treacherous coast and the sails would carry her across the Pacific without need to store large quantities of fuel. She would be small enough to maneuver into the hideaway bays that Kohler knew along the coast, yet large enough, too, to bring in a heavy load of aliens and opium across the ocean.

They had chosen a suitable ship. But buying a ship is not in itself illegal—and the most I could do was to obtain a complete list of the names of the crew, with photos, to distribute to our agents in preparation for the time when the *Hedwig* might return, possibly loaded with contraband.

On July 30th, Ypma signed his clearance papers and headed for the open sea. He gave his destination as China, his cargo as ballast. Kohler and Rumbler were passengers.

I heard the news with mingled feelings of interest and doubt. Possibly one of this country's biggest smuggling cases had started, indistinct as yet but gradually emerging.

I wired Washington complete details. Gorman instructed me to contact M. R. Nicholson, a veteran Treasury attaché in Shanghai. He had been in this service for years and knew Shanghai as well as his home town. So I sent him our information and he went to work at once.

Nicholson quickly dug up some additional facts:

First, in Macao, he learned that a broker named Wong Sui who lived in Soochow had purchased 1,750 five-tael cans of gum opium.

Then, in Shanghai, through his undercover agents, he learned that Chan Choy, a Chinese slave trader, had circulated the news that he could take about seventy Chinese to the United States upon guarantee of $1,000 each. Also, he said he was in the market for good buys in "pretty women". Chan had visited the Yee Tsui dive and tried to bargain for seven of their most comely prostitutes. While smuggling women is far more dangerous because they are more easily discovered, it is three times as profitable. The girls could be bought from their Oriental owners for a few dollars and sold in America for $3,000 each to wealthy Chinese.

Finally, Nicholson reported that on September 24 the *Hedwig* hove into the port of Woosung, nearly forty miles above Shanghai.

Ypma reported to the registry division to declare his ship and make preparations for a clearance to his next destination, which was declared to be Cocos Island, for pearl fishing. In the meantime, Kohler had left the *Hedwig* to make arrangements in Shanghai for contraband. The report did not mention George Rumbler. We never knew what happened to him, as he did not appear in this case again.

When I heard of the Cocos Island being the ship's declared destination, my respect for Ypma's resourcefulness went up. It was a clever plan. The Dutchman could go out to sea, meet a Chinese junk, pick up the cargo of opium and aliens and sail straight for the West Coast. After unloading her contraband, the ship could then go to Cocos Island and return to Shanghai without losing her registry.

As it worked out, it was even better than that.

There is an island, Tsung Wing, squarely in the middle of the Yangtze above Woosung. Instead of going straight down the river and loading its illicit cargo at sea, the *Hedwig*, on the orders of wily old Wong Quai Sun, used this island as a natural screen to conceal her movements and change of course.

The schooner headed for the open sea on the afternoon of September 27th, apparently off on her "pearl fishing" expedition. Then, as darkness fell, the canvas dropped from the masts and the powerful engines roared into action as Ypma reversed his course and steamed back upstream to the far side of the island of Tsung Wing. There, out of sight of Woosung, he ordered the anchor dropped.

All next day the *Hedwig* rode at anchor. Then, as night fell and darkness again covered the Yangtze, Captain Ypma took his position on the bridge and ordered full speed ahead. He knew the schooner must make the trip up the Yangtze to Kiangyin, load her cargo and return to the island before dawn, as Wong Quai Sun had ordered. And the distance was over fifty miles. With doused lights they moved upriver at top speed, until from the starboard came a blinding light from a big junk. Ypma, flashing the white light on the for-

ward mast of the *Hedwig*, ordered, "Slow . . . . reverse
. . . . stop!"

Aboard the junk a Chinese scrambled up the mast like a
monkey and swung a lighted lantern three times in an arc. A
few minutes later, three huge sampans, sculled by sweating
coolies, came from the shore. Their bamboo bumpers scraped
against the schooner's side.

Jacob's ladders were dropped from the *Hedwig*'s decks,
and yellow men scrambled up with sacks slung over their
backs. As the sacks were piled high there was a dull clunk as
lead containers of opium struck one upon the other. Then the
human cargo climbed the ladders.

Kohler had come aboard. He ordered the sacks stowed
in the forward hatch, the Chinese men herded below. The
seven girls were put into a cabin. The whole operation took
less than an hour.

Captain Ypma swung the vessel around and headed
back. Dawn was beginning to break as the anchor chain
clanked through the hawse hole at the island refuge. One
more day of waiting—then the loaded *Hedwig* set out for the
Pacific coast of America.

Meanwhile, in San Francisco, Customs was getting a reception party ready.

A coded wire from Nicholson reached us October 14th:
HEDWIG LEFT SHANGHAI IN BALLAST FOR CO-
COS ISLAND ON 27th. RELIABLY INFORMED WHEN
TWENTY MILES OFF WOOSUNG SHE RETURNED
YANGTZE RIVER AND MET CHINESE JUNK. SEV-
ENTY CHINESE MEN AND SEVEN CHINESE GIRLS
AND ONE THOUSAND SEVEN HUNDRED FIFTY
CANS OF OPIUM PUT ON BOARD. BELIEVE HEAD-
ING FOR CALIFORNIA. STOWAWAYS IN CHARGE OF
CHIN HOY. WILL INFORM YOU LATER IF LEARN
NEW DEVELOPMENTS.

We figured the trip would take the *Hedwig* from twenty to thirty-five days, depending on luck and the weather. She might arrive in a few days or a few weeks. This gave all of us considerable worry. My nights were almost sleepless.

Though I did not know it then, Gene Kohler was having some worries, too.

Twenty days out of Shanghai, food and water supplies began to run low. The cramped holds of the ship had no decent accommodations for the human cargo that had been jammed into them. As rations and water grew short, there came a fierce rumbling from the confined men.

"Keep them all below," Kohler ordered the guard. "We can't take chances on the devils swarming us to get at the grub and water tanks."

So the cries, the curses and threats of the hungry Chinese went unanswered. Day by day their thirst and starvation mounted.

On the twenty-fifth day out, Chin Hoy, in charge of the prisoners, was lowering pails of sticky rice and a scant supply of brackish water into the hold through a crack in the hatch covering when, with a wild yell, a half dozen gaunt Chinese forced their way to the deck.

Kohler shouted to the thugs who made up the crew. They caught up belaying pins and rushed toward the unarmed prisoners. Swinging their clubs, they beat the yelling Chinese into insensibility and flung them back into the hold.

Kohler ordered Chin Hoy: "Tell those heathen brothers of yours that this is just a sample of what they'll get if they try anything else."

That night the lamentations from the men below decks drowned out the whistle of wind through the rigging. By morning two of the prisoners were dead. Kohler had their bodies thrown overboard without any burial service.

Chin Hoy protested the unnecessary deaths. "These men

worth thousan' dollar. Only t'ree hunded paid now each one. We lose seven hunded when one man die", he said in poor English.

"I don't give a damn how many of them die!" Kohler cursed. "I didn't want to take them in the first place. Wong Quai Sun argued me into it. We could have taken more dope and made more money."

When Chin Hoy continued to protest, Kohler threatened to throw him overboard, also.

The Chinese girls in the cabin, however, fared differently. They had plenty of food and all the comforts that the ship afforded. Kohler had stocked the ship with liquor in China and, at times during the voyage, he shared part of it with the women.

Below decks, conditions steadily got worse. All the prisoners might have died if it had not been for Ypma who, whenever possible, instructed Chin Hoy to pass down extra rations of rice and water.

While they were still two days' journey from the American coast, one of the prisoners, crazed from hunger, thirst and the stifling heat under the deck, tried to set fire to the ship. Kohler and the crew hastily dumped seawater into the hold to extinguish the blaze. The men below, their tongues parched from thirst, lapped at the salt water.

Kohler cursed and prodded the Captain to make more speed.

"Two days," said Ypma. "Two days and I'll be putting her into Mack's Arch, Oregon, for you. Give those poor devils below something to eat and drink. We've got plenty left for two days."

So the Chinese were fed, and the wailing stopped.

Meanwhile, on shore, one Lewis Baker of San Francisco was busily at work preparing for the landing. In China,

Nicholson had intercepted cables from Baker to Kohler and sent us copies. They were in a code we could not decipher. Nevertheless, we began to shadow Baker.

We Customs officers had found it impossible to cover the entire sixteen hundred miles of coast line from Canada to Mexico, but we had been watching most of the strategic points. The Coast Guard patrols, the lightships, and Customs were all working together, all with assignments to go into effect the instant the *Hedwig* was sighted.

About this time the Federal Communications Commission handed us a report on a wildcat radio station in the vicinity of Richmond, California, across the bay from San Francisco. The station was sending out coded messages every evening at eleven o'clock.

The radio experts had a finding apparatus mounted on a truck. After locating the wave length of the unlicensed station, they circled it, gradually cutting down the size of the circle to reach the center. But again the crafty operators frustrated us. The sending station was also mounted on a truck. By moving its position between short broadcasts, the sending truck was able to elude the finding device. And though we were convinced the station was sending messages to the *Hedwig*, we were unable to decipher them.

Mack's Arch, Oregon, was perhaps the last place on the coast we would expect Kohler to go ashore. It is a long way from San Francisco, where the Chinese were apparently to be taken, and it is a dangerous spot to navigate. A group of rocks forms a partly submerged reef in front of a narrow strip of beach that bends into a shallow bay. There is a winding, crooked course for piloting a ship close inshore, with less than six fathoms of water between the sharp reefs on either side.

To make it seem even less feasible as a landing place,

there was no road from the beach to the highway which runs along the coast several miles from the ocean.

While the *Hedwig* was making her round trip across the Pacific, though, Lewis Baker had been taking care of this detail. Under the guise of cutting wood, he made a narrow truck trail to the beach. He even built portable bridges and had them in readiness to set up on a day's notice to cross creeks and ravines.

Our entire force was on the alert. Likewise, every coastal trading ship with a radio was asked to check on their routes for a sight of the *Hedwig*. We thought we had a good chance of seizing the ship and its contraband—that is, until on the very day the *Hedwig* seemed certain to make shore, a thick fog descended on the coast.

It was one of those breaks we couldn't foresee. It seemed tough.

"Perhaps," we told each other, "Ypma will ride out the fog instead of taking a chance on getting beached."

For two days we hopefully told ourselves that. Then a heavy storm blew in along the coast. Lighthouses, lightships, Coast Guard vessels, our own small boats—none were able to locate the *Hedwig*.

For weeks we continued to search for Kohler and Ypma. We had no way of knowing whether they had landed or not. Then, early in November, a fisherman from Rogue River came into Crescent City, California, with a motor tender in tow behind his fishing schooner. He had picked it up adrift near Mack's Arch just after the storm. The tender was from the *Hedwig!*

So—we had failed.

Kohler had landed his first cargo, one of the richest loads of dope and aliens ever to reach the United States, and we had not caught him.

We did the one thing left. Raiding squads of Customs and Immigration officers were sent to rip apart San Francisco's Chinatown. Shops and homes of every person on the list of Wong Tai's visitors, as well as many others, were turned upside down.

We got much of the opium and five of the aliens, nothing more.

There was nothing to do but wait for the next load—and hope for success.

The *Hedwig*, however, was on her way to disaster.

She had made a successful landing, due partly to Captain Ypma's amazing skill in taking a boat through a reef, and also to Kohler's accurate knowledge of the coast. She had pulled up right in front of Mack's Arch in what must have been a remarkable feat of navigation and seamanship.

There they anchored. Baker was waiting at the beach with a fleet of covered trucks, with casks of fresh water and supplies of food. As the aliens and opium were brought ashore in the tenders, the water and provisions were loaded aboard for the return voyage.

But the storm blew in before they had finished reloading the *Hedwig*. The barometer began dropping rapidly.

"We've got to pull out," the Captain told Kohler. "If the anchors give way we'll be caught on the reef!"

Ypma gave orders to put out to sea. The last of the shore boats was hurriedly tied to the stern instead of being hoisted to the deck.

As the Captain gave the ship full power, a wave caught the trailing tender, swiped it sideways and broke it loose from the line.

That, of course, was the tender recovered by the Rogue River fisherman.

The *Hedwig* set her course for China. Kohler wanted to

collect his share of the profits and prepare for the next trip. They dropped down to the South China Sea so they could come back up the coast and give the impression that they were returning from their pearl fishing expedition to Cocos Island.

While they were off the coast of south China, a terrific storm came up. Before they could haul down their canvas, the mainmast snapped and covered the deck with splintered timbers. Other sails were ripped, the rigging fouled. The Captain ordered the engineer to put on the auxiliary power. But one mast was still under canvas. It caught the full force of the wind, making the engines useless. The ship heeled over in a trough and shipped enough water to make her logy.

Calls for help went out by radio. The British naval cruiser Suffolk, out of Hong Kong, answered the *Hedwig*'s SOS. The cruiser rescued Kohler, Ypma and the crew, but the battered schooner was abandoned to the mercy of the sea.

Back in San Francisco, we were informed by Treasury Attaché Nicholson that the smugglers were safely in Hong Kong.

"What now?" was a logical question for us. We could, of course, try to extradite them and bring them before a grand jury. But, in spite of what we knew about their activities, we still had few tangible facts that could be used as legal evidence. Finally, in view of the great expense involved in bringing them back to stand trial, and the small chance that we had of obtaining convictions, we decided to wait and see what their next move would be.

For a long time nothing happened. Nicholson kept Ypma and Kohler under constant surveillance, while we on the Pacific coast went on to other investigations.

Months later, word reached us that Ypma and Kohler had ordered built for them a teakwood ship, 125 feet long, with a 200 horsepower diesel engine. She was being readied in Yaumati shipyard, in China, and the name plate across the stern announced that she was the *Marbella*.

A certain Karl Beitzer, German by birth, had been hired as engineer and radio operator. Once more, a smuggling venture apparently was getting underway.

This time, though, we had an advantage. During the long lull in operations, our men had broken the code.

That was how we discovered one of a series of double, triple, and quadruple crosses that were to make the *Marbella* case infamous even in the annals of smuggling.

By coded cable, Gene Kohler bargained with a connection in San Francisco to sell 3,800 cans of opium for $200,000.

Since we knew that Wong Quai Sun's broker had purchased this exact amount of opium to be shipped on the *Marbella*, and that Kohler's part in the affair was merely to get the cargo furnished by the Wongs across the ocean, it became clear that he was trying to deal independently.

The *Marbella* slid down the ways in due time, registered under the flag of Panama. Next day the brokers for the aliens were notified to have their men and women assembled on the top floor of Number 145 Queen's Road, Hong Kong, at 6 p.m.

Four days later Nicholson sent the following message:

"Auxiliary motor schooner *Marbella* slipped away from Hong Kong at 2 a.m. in ballast. Vessel painted dull blue all over. Suspect she will carry 130 stowaways and 20,000 cans opium to San Francisco, landing at points unknown. All Pacific naval stations notified to be on lookout and inform your office by wireless."

The following day we got another cable telling us that the *Marbella* and the stowaways had failed to make contact on the high seas, and that the aliens had been returned to Hong Kong.

The next day I received a third cable, confirming the

previous one: "*Marbella* sailed without stowaways or opium arranged for by Wong Quai Sun. Will try to learn what happened."

Later I found out about the aliens. Lok Po Shan, the stowaway master, had pocketed the three hundred dollars advanced by each of the passengers.

That was the first double cross.

The matter of Wong Quai Sun's opium was the second. That had been arranged by Wong Tai. He had sought out Kohler as the *Marbella* was nearing completion and told him that since it was he, Wong Tai, who had the United States contacts for selling the opium, he would furnish his own stuff for Kohler to deliver to a different company than the one Wong Quai Sun had bargained with. The profits would then be split two ways instead of three. Sun's opium, and aliens as well, would be left behind.

Kohler objected, at first. Old Wong Quai Sun would take vengeance when the *Marbella* returned to China. But Wong Tai declared that his uncle was old and sick, and would "be with his ancestors" by the time the vessel returned.

So Kohler agreed—outwardly. Inwardly, he was wondering why, if Wong Quai Sun was going to his ancestors, Gene Kohler alone might not profit on it. Also, after the trouble on board the *Hedwig*, Kohler was glad to dispense with the aliens.

Consequently, he wired Baker to find a customer on the Pacific coast, then had Wong Tai's opium loaded aboard the *Marbella*. This was why the schooner had not picked up Wong Quai's aliens and opium at sea.

Nicholson had planted an informer as one of the aliens. He reported that the junk had waited at sea a hundred miles out to make connection with the *Marbella*. When the schooner had not appeared after three days, the junk brought its cargo of 130 aliens and 20,000 cans of opium back to China.

So the *Marbella* sailed toward the United States.

Kohler figured, after this trip, to take the Marbella to the East coast, safely away from the tong's vengeance, and run liquor from the Bahamas. When he told Ypma of this plan, the Dutchman objected:

"The minute the ship reaches the Canal, the authorities will seize her!"

But Kohler had an answer: "We'll go around the Horn."

On the American side of the Pacific, we of the Customs Service were waiting.

We organized a coast patrol two weeks before the vessel could possibly arrive. Men were stationed at lookout points so that every bay or possible landing point from Canada to Mexico was covered.

Again we had the lighthouse keepers, lightships and the Coast Guard on watch, all supplied with photos of the *Marbella*. The State Highway patrols and Agricultural Inspection stations agreed to help by blocking the highways and state borders in the event the *Marbella* should reach the shore and try to move her cargo by truck. The Navy Pacific Command had their aircraft carriers and destroyers, then practicing war maneuvers along the coast, on the lookout.

Finally, we had the *Marbella*'s Panamanian registry cancelled. This made her an illegal ship, liable to seizure by any government at any time she was sighted.

As an added precaution, we organized daily airplane patrols over the ocean at San Francisco, San Diego and Seattle.

Each day the planes would fly ninety miles out to sea, then swoop up and down the coast for some sight of the schooner. Yet they had no luck. With her dull blue paint that closely matched the ocean, she was difficult to find.

In August, the San Francisco radio station KUP picked up a message from the motorship *Reliance* that it had spotted the *Marbella* in Turtle Bay, Mexico. The Coast

Guard cutter *Bonham* was sent under full speed to the location. But the *Marbella* apparently had intercepted the *Reliance's* message and sailed away.

She might be on her way to the United States.

Baker, meanwhile, had radioed Kohler to stay well away from the coast. He had arranged to use a small, fast boat, the *Redwood*, to make contact in the first heavy fog. So when, early in September, a layer of fog covered the coast, Baker and several helpers sped out of the Golden Gate and put out to sea.

They met the *Marbella*. Four thousand cans of opium were transferred to the smaller craft.

Before Kohler came in with the load, he told Ypma to go back to Turtle Bay and wait. After selling the opium, Kohler said, he would meet Ypma there and give him enough money to buy supplies and charts for the trip around the Horn. Then Kohler would cross the country by train and make arrangements in Florida for disposal of future rum cargoes.

Hidden by the fog, the *Redwood* made a landing at Stimson Beach in spite of all our vigilance. The cans were buried in the sand until Kohler could find a buyer.

Kohler had eluded Customs again—but a surprise awaited him. He couldn't sell his opium. He couldn't even give it away!

Not a broker in San Francisco or any other place in the entire United States would touch a can of it.

The Wong family had issued an ultimatum. With a triple-cross Kohler had tricked Wong Tai, and a ban had been placed on his opium.

All that the Wongs had to show for the money they had spent for the *Hedwig* and the building of the *Marbella* were the profits from the aliens and opium landed on the Oregon coast from the *Hedwig*. The other aliens were holding them responsible for the money Lok Po Shan had stolen. Their friends and relatives were demanding the return of the money they had paid for the venture.

Kohler spent his own money and all he could borrow, trying to find a taker. He was as penniless as the day he had left the penitentiary.

Lewis Baker made the quadruple cross of this case. He abandoned Kohler to the Wongs' mercy when Kohler could not dispose of the narcotics.

Aboard the *Marbella*, Captain Ypma also ran into misfortune. After the *Reliance* revealed his Turtle Bay hideout, he could no longer drop an anchor there. Off the Mexican coast near the Cedros Islands, the Mexican gunboat SAF II overhauled the *Marbella* and boarded her. The SAF's Captain told him he was wanted for smuggling, and searched the ship. Though the Mexicans found no contraband, they imposed a fine which took almost all the cash Ypma had. Then they radioed the schooner's position.

The Coast Guard cutters *Bonham* and *Ewing* were sent to the Cedros Islands, one to take the left side of the main island, the other cutter the right. While the two vessels were heading under full speed to the Cedros, arrangements were made by Agent Rae Vader for a high-powered amateur radio sending station to operate on the wave length Baker had been using. Vader had the operator direct the *Marbella* to stay in her position and to say that Kohler was coming to her assistance.

It looked like a perfect plan, but again the hard luck that had plagued us all through this case overtook us. As the cutters were passing San Diego, the radio operator of the *Ewing* was stricken with appendicitis and the cutter had to put in to port.

The *Bonham* continued on to Cedros, but the moment she was sighted the *Marbella* pulled up anchor and started away. The giant engines in the outlaw ship drove her so fast that the Coast Guard never got within firing range.

For a month we heard nothing. Then we got the news that the British government had seized the ship as Ypma tried to make harbor at Hong Kong. The confiscated *Marbella* was turned over to the Chinese Navy.

That smuggling venture was ended—but not as we of Customs had hoped.

Ypma and his engineer, Karl Beitzer, were stranded in China without a cent between them.

Kohler and Baker were broke in San Francisco.

Wong Tai and Wong Quai Sun—who had not joined his ancestors on schedule after all—were in debt to friends and relatives.

Nicholson interviewed Ypma and Beitzer in China. They gave him a detailed account of the *Marbella's* smuggling operations. They were in a mood to testify against the others involved in the scheme, so our Treasury Attaché arranged for them to come to the United States as prospective witnesses.

Meeting them on their arrival in Seattle, I took them to U.S. Attorney George Hatfield in San Francisco. He had them testify before the Federal grand jury there. True bills were returned against all individuals known to be connected with the *Marbella* case.

After first arranging for the safe detention of Ypma and Beitzer until the case could be tried, we began looking for the other defendants.

Wong Quai Sun and Wong Tai, in China, were out of our jurisdiction. So the search centered on Kohler and Baker.

A short time later, the headlines of the morning papers told us exactly where to find Baker.

The night before, he had been killed in American gangster style while driving his car down the Bayshore highway. Both he and his car had been riddled with bullets.

Then we devoted all our efforts to locating Kohler. We knew from his previous record that he had a wife and baby daughter. The girl should now be of school age.

We checked hundreds of school records in the San Francisco area and eventually found what we were looking for, including Mrs. Kohler's address.

We did not know whether she was on good terms with her husband, so a roundabout approach was necessary.

Our plan was to have a clever woman operative develop an acquaintance with Mrs. Kohler. After a time they became so friendly that they rented an apartment together. In a few days we learned that Mrs. Kohler herself did not know where her husband was. She had been trying to find him for two years, to force him to support his daughter.

All our attempts to locate Kohler for trial failed. We tried every possible means.

Four years later, we finally learned why he could not be found.

About the time that Baker was killed American-style, it appeared that Kohler had died Chinese style. In March, 1936, the bones of Kohler's skeleton, bound with wire, were found in San Mateo County near San Francisco. Several rolls of wire had been twisted around his throat—a typical Chinese execution. Identification was definitely established from dental work records at McNeil Island penitentiary, where Kohler had met Wong Tai.

So the smugglers' loot, the fortune in gum opium first dreamed of in a Federal penitentiary and transported across the seas in the *Marbella*, still lies buried, we believe, somewhere beneath the sands or in the waters of the Pacific shore.

The Mexican Border

EXPERIENCE HAS TAUGHT US of the Customs Service that smuggling is not limited to seaports or gates of entry at international borders and airports. This is especially true of the Mexican border, which is partly Rio Grande river and partly desert sand, sagebrush and cacti, 1,549 miles of it.

My acquaintance with the Mexican border began one autumn when we heard that a load of heroin was to start moving across the line. Our information on this was sketchy, and as we found out later, some of the narcotics got through. Fortunately for us, the smugglers' El Paso outlets were not as smoothly run as was their supply base. Somebody fumbled and they ended up in our hands in time. Then we learned how clever were some of their tricks.

Mexican dope smugglers did not operate on a huge scale, differing from the Oriental smuggling organizations which were—and are—well-organized and efficient. Usually there were groups of only four or five who conspired to get their contraband across the border. Sometimes a lone smuggler would try. But many separate groups operating along a boundary of more than fifteen hundred miles was, and is, a mammoth and difficult problem for the United States. The

34

efforts of the United States government jointly with the Mexican government, stepped-up in 1969, to detect and halt narcotics coming across the common border, is as much as can be done until the supply sources have been cut off.

Since opium and marijuana have been for years the single money crop for many Mexican farmers, the immense difficulty of the task is obvious.

The Customs officers regularly stationed along the Mexican border had some ingenious ways of running down smugglers. One, called "trail-cutting", meant studying a given area for signs that someone had crossed during the night.

If there were tracks, some of the men in the patrol could tell, by the type of insects crushed by the walker's heel, whether the crossing had occurred before or after midnight.

They could tell by the way the dew had settled in the tracks how early in the evening it had been.

Like the early Indians, they could gauge the weight of the traveler and the probable load he carried.

One group that was eventually tracked down used to shoe their horses backwards. After a while we learned to get off our own mounts and study the hoofprints. The way the sand had been scuffed up would usually reveal the trick. But until we got on to it, we usually went trotting off in the direction from which they had come, instead of the way they were going.

That made for considerable confusion before we finally caught the men. We also confiscated their horses—which immediately were shod correctly and put into a more legitimate service.

Another group used horses to even better advantage:

A horse will always go back to a place where he has habitually been fed. For many nights in succession these men waded their horses across the shallow part of the river and fed them on the United States side.

One night, when there was no moon, these men loaded

their horses' saddlebags with oilskin-wrapped packages of heroin, turned them loose on the Mexican side and watched while the animals went straight to the place where they had been fed across the stream.

Hidden American confederates on the other side watched, too. When no Customs men appeared, they walked boldly down to the horses, took out the contents of the saddlebags and gave the animals the oats they were waiting for.

Many of the patrolmen were shot while working on the border. Snipers hidden across the river would wait for the moment when the Customs man was most vulnerable. Later patrols would find him there—face buried in the tracks he had been studying.

There is an intense, lasting anger that comes over an enforcement officer when one of his fellow workers is shot down while performing his necessary duty.

An Agent named Baker found his partner that way one morning and swore vengeance.

"I'll get the fellows who did that, I promise you."

He set his plans carefully. He knew his movements were always watched, that his routine had been figured out and anticipated. Now he began to emphasize the regularity of his behavior. He made a point of driving his car down to the river on a last-moment inspection, getting out and walking along the shore, then driving away to put the car in the garage and casually go home.

He resisted all temptation to return unexpectedly. A few smugglers might get across before he was ready. But he was after the big operators he knew were guilty.

One night Baker decided the time had come. He called his son into action. The boy was a husky young fellow, and his father's uniform fit him well.

Baker crouched down in the back of the car and let his son drive. When they reached the river, the young man in his father's uniform got out, walked back and forth for a while, and then returned to the car. Meanwhile, Baker carefully and silently opened the door on the side of the car away from the river, rolled out into a clump of mesquite, and quickly hid himself. He had his flashlight, his automatic and his handcuffs, prepared to surprise some big-time smugglers.

The son drove off, according to plan.

Something went wrong. Maybe the dope runners saw Baker roll out of the car. Maybe there was a difference in the son's movements that tipped off the smugglers. We never knew what it was. The next morning the youth went out to bring back his father. He found him dead—of a bullet wound through the head.

Many of those smugglers who were convicted and sentenced spent less time in prison than the time officers had spent in catching them. Some of them may again be trying to wade horses across the Rio Grande, especially with today's intensified inspection at the ports of entry.

Just before the beginning of World War II, as diplomatic relations between the United States and Japan deteriorated steadily, U.S. officers increased their surveillance of vessels arriving from the Orient. This brought added problems to smugglers who relied on their supplies of contraband from Oriental vessels putting in at Pacific coast ports.

A Chinese narcotics smuggler of Seattle, faced by this situation, decided to try to establish purchasing connections in Mexico.

He duly arrived in Culiacan, state of Sinaloa, Mexico, and was successful in buying a load of smoking opium, which he put in his car and started for the border. He had gone about twenty miles when he was stopped by men in uniform who declared they were officers. They seized the narcotics but returned it to him at once when he paid them a large sum of money.

When he had gone another fifty miles or so, the same thing happened again. The alleged officers released him and his cargo when he offered them money also.

Finally, just before he reached the U.S. border at Nogales, Sonora, he was arrested by Mexican officers, fined a large amount of money, and both his car and the narcotics confiscated.

Upon his return to Seattle, the Chinese held a meeting of his associates and advised them that the Mexicans were dishonest, did not do business like the Chinese, and could not be trusted. With great indignation, he said to me: "All Mexican clooked—no can trust!"

This particular Chinese acted as an informer for me on occasion when he was in a position to inform on his competitors to his own advantage. When he could learn anything about the plans or activities of his rival smugglers, he came to me. While not admitting it was he who made the buying trip to Mexico which ended in misfortune for him, he told me at great length about someone he knew who had undergone these unhappy experiences. If I had not already known that it was he, himself, who had been subjected to such treatment, his naive, innocent manner might have fooled me entirely. The Oriental has few equals in wary, deceptive methods.

After this experience, the Chinese narcotic smugglers, all of whom seemed to hear of it immediately, would stay on the American side of the Mexican border and demand that the seller bring the contraband across before he would be paid.

❖ ❖ ❖ ❖ ❖ ❖ ❖ ❖

World War II disrupted the narcotic smuggling syndicates dealing both with Europe and the Orient.

In the interim big and small dealers tried to establish connections with Mexico, which had the capabilities of producing narcotics in larger quantities than before.

After the war, these operations, now well-established, continued to be active.

Early in 1947, the Supervising Customs Agent and the Federal Narcotic Agent-in-Charge in Los Angeles received information that large amounts of illicit narcotic drugs were being sold to American wholesale dealers in the area of Mexicali, Mexico. The drugs were being smuggled across the border by Mexican sellers for delivery to American buyers.

A Federal Narcotic Agent named Ben Stevenson, experienced in making big "buys" from illicit dealers, was sent to Calexico, California, directly across the border from Mexicali, where he took up headquarters in a motel. Joe Sheehan and Al Smith, two Customs Agents experienced also in anti-narcotic smuggling work, moved into a different motel in Calexico where they could be reached quickly by Stevenson should a case develop.

The case that later materialized was called by us the "Battle By The American Canal."

Working undercover, Narcotic Agent Stevenson soon became acquainted with a big dealer in Mexico and began the necessary haggling over price and point of delivery.

A genuine dealer in illicit drugs always tries to get the best price and will haggle and bargain for days and sometimes even for weeks. After the price has been agreed on, then jockeying usually begins as to place and method of delivery of the contraband and how the payment will be made.

Stevenson was an expert at his job. After three weeks of talks and meetings with the Mexican suppliers, he was advised by them to remain in his motel for the next three days and have the money ready. During that three days they would call on him and would take him at that time to the point of delivery which, as the agent "buyer" had insisted, would be on the American side of the border.

The money was paid at time of delivery, but the Mexican would have to see the money first at the motel.

This presented problems for the officers. If the delivery were to be made in the daytime, the surrounding area, being flat and open, did not provide much opportunity for concealment of the officers to assist in any possible arrests.

The three agents made the best arrangements they could under the circumstances.

Agent Stevenson was to advise the smugglers when they arrived that he had left the money elsewhere, and they were to return in two hours when he would have it for them and be ready to receive the contraband.

This explanation would be plausible to the dealers because no experienced crook ever keeps large amounts of money on or near him during the buying arrangements for fear of robbery or double cross by the sellers.

These plans would make it possible for the two Customs Agents, Smith and Sheehan, fully armed, to be hidden in the trunk of the car. This would assure their presence nearby without the risk of following the car in open country. Such following might tip off the entire arrangement, especially if the transaction were to be made in daylight.

Stevenson, Sheehan and Smith had held a practice session early. Among the available cars, they looked for one with an adequate trunk.

"Remember, there are two of us to hide in that thing, and it'll be hot as hades," said Sheehan dubiously.

Stevenson pointed to a big black sedan.

"This one ought to do. You two might even have room enough to fan each other," he joked.

A Customs patrolman named Francis Merkt was well acquainted with all the roads and fields in that entire area, and also was thoroughly experienced in handling smugglers. He was alerted to be ready to follow at a considerable distance if the opportunity arose. This proved to be the plan that saved the day because this patrolman was a sharpshooter with a rifle. He had served in the Philippines invasion during World War II and had had a great deal of experience.

On the second day of the three-day period that Stevenson was told to stay in his motel, Barbo, the Mexican dealer, came to the motel at one o'clock in the afternoon. He said he was ready to make delivery and wanted to see the money.

"Come back in two hours, Barbo, and the money will be here," the Agent told him.

Some time after his departure, Stevenson notified the two Customs Agents. They went to the car and got in the trunk, fully armed. The three had planned that when the contraband was presented and payment demanded in full, Stevenson was to say, "I've got the money in the trunk." As he unlocked it, the Customs men were to jump out and, with the Narcotic Agent, arrest the smugglers.

A neat arrangement—but such arrangements with racketeers don't always work out as planned.

At 3 p.m. the Mexican dealer returned to complete the deal. He was shown some money by Stevenson. Barbo took the roll of bills and counted them quickly, then scowled.

"Only two thousand here. Where's the rest? You tryin' to cheat?" he demanded.

"Don't blow your lid," answered the Agent. "The rest is in the car—all of it—and I'll pay you when you give me the load and I see it's the real article."

Still scowling, Barbo got into the car with Stevenson and, unknown to the Mexican, of course, Agents Sheehan and Smith. He directed Stevenson to drive west along a country road near the border. They finally arrived at a large irrigation canal leading from the Colorado river, known as the American Canal. The Mexican border was about two hundred feet away.

There, waiting in the tall grass, were two Mexicans with gunny sacks. The Agent noticed that both men were armed, one with a sub-machine gun, the other with a revolver. Also, just over the line in Mexico, not over 250 feet away, stood another Mexican armed with a machine gun, quite plainly there to cover the transaction.

Stevenson demanded to see and test the narcotics. Taking out his vial of acid and special paper for the purpose, he tested a generous amount and found it to be genuine.

While doing this, he said in a voice loud enough for the concealed Customs Agents to overhear:

"You don't need these men with those pistols and machine guns. I'm *bueno!*"

"Well, I gotta be sure," answered Barbo, frowning.

Then Stevenson said, "Everything seems OK. I'll unlock the back end. I've got the money in the trunk."

When he unlocked the trunk, Smith and Sheehan pushed up the lid and came out in a hurry with drawn guns. No one, however, had anticipated the effect on their eyes when emerging from the darkness of the trunk into the bright sunshine of a Mexican border afternoon.

At first, their eyes were so blinded they could see nothing. During the split second it took the Mexicans to realize the situation, Stevenson quickly pushed the two Customs men toward the other side of the car and darted after them.

Shouts and brittle Spanish exclamations broke out.

The nearest Mexicans opened up on the car with machine gun and revolver fire, trying to hit the Agents on the other side. The machine gun nearest the car soon jammed. But the Agents were more concerned with the machine gunner just over the Mexican line, because he was moving around to a point where the car would not interfere with his line of fire.

The Agents seemed trapped until suddenly they heard a high-powered rifle "speak up" from the American side near them and saw the machine gunner across the line pitch backward, dropping the gun. At this, the two other Mexicans and Barbo began a run for the border. One was dropped by someone on our side, as all the Agents were now firing. Barbo managed to crawl across the border line where he was immune to arrest by our officers.

Merkt walked up from his place of concealment. The other officers in the fray were more than grateful to him for using his rifle so expertly.

Our officers confiscated a large amount of narcotics. The body of the car was flayed with bullet holes and the windshield peppered. I saw it when it was sent to Los Angeles for repairs, and I couldn't see how any of the men not only came out alive, but were not even wounded.

Some one in Mexico apparently felt he had been double crossed by the Chief of Police of Mexicali. On the afternoon of the following day, the Mexican official was shot to death while driving his jeep from his home to his office.

So ended the "Battle By The American Canal."

The Chin Shieu Case

IT WAS A WARM AUTUMN DAY ON the island of Oahu.

Into the Customs office in Honolulu came a teamster named Yung Bark Yau, with a pickup order for twelve cases of dried fruit. There was nothing extraordinary about that. It happened often.

To the Customs Inspector, this order was slightly different from the usual one. Out of a shipment of sixty-nine cases, the order called for only twelve—and of those twelve, none of the numbers was consecutive.

The Inspector pondered this while the warehouseman wheeled out the cases to the loading platform. Then, just before the grinning teamster claimed his load, the Customs man, following his hunch, stepped forward, ripped off the dry board cover of the topmost box, and shoved a steel testing rod down into the dried fruit.

The rod struck metal. Yung Bark Yau grunted and began to back away.

"Hold him," the Inspector told his men, and went on probing. The box yielded 275 five-tael tin cans of opium. The other eleven cases brought the total to 3,339 cans, worth a small fortune.

"A cut-and-dried case," you would think. "Smuggler caught with the goods, the names of both shipper and receiver on the records—pure routine!"

Yet, consider what happened.

The Federal Grand Jury returned two indictments against the obvious people—Chin Shieu, manager of the Yee Lung Tai Company, and the truck driver, Yung Bark Yau.

The defendants were brought to trial on one indictment. They were acquitted. The remaining indictment, considered the weaker of the two, was not brought to trial immediately but was allowed to remain on the books.

Almost two years after the seizure of the opium, I was assigned to Honolulu. My instructions were to attempt to develop the facts further so that the U.S. attorney could either proceed to trial, or recommend dismissal of the indictment.

This case—known as the Chin Shieu—was to keep me busy for months and, in addition, give me a practical course in Chinese theology that I never forgot.

Cop and robber stories usually start out with fanfare. They usually end that way, too. That's not true of real-life sleuthing. All my big cases started small, and though there might be gun-blasting at times, the hours of excitement were counter-balanced by weeks and even months of monotonous routine investigations.

And finding the guilty person was only half of it. We had to have proof of his guilt. The Federal government demands very precise evidence and it also requires its agents to secure this evidence through lawful means. No entrapment, no unlawful entry, nothing was allowed that would violate the right of the citizen to maintain his privacy. Anything different could establish the basis for a police state. Still, there have been times when I—and a host of other government men—spent months and even years finding the proof necessary to convict a person who everyone in enforcement circles had known was guilty from the moment the crime was discovered.

I had tangled with Chinese dope smugglers enough to understand the big gap between guessing and proving their guilt. I knew how an Oriental could backtrack and double-trail and how his relatives and friends would enter the picture to save him. I went to Hawaii with misgivings. Sometimes I think I'd still be there, following rag-ends of clues if, about a month after my arrival in Honolulu, Chin Shieu had not committed suicide.

At first thought, this seemed like a blow against us. A man who might have cracked under questioning had gone to his ancestors with his lips sealed. Nor is it a Chinese custom for a suicide to leave a note! Yet, he did something for us, after all.

At the coroner's inquest, Chong Ho, Chin Shieu's widow, testified that just before he cut his throat, Chin Shieu had sought out a group photograph hanging on the living room wall and marked a great red X across a man's face.

This could have been significant. When questioned further, however, the widow answered reluctantly, "That's all my husband tell me."

It was up to me to find the proof that would back up the U.S. attorney's case. And the only real lead I had was the X that Chin Shieu had marked over the face in the photograph.

Hoping to learn more, I went to see Chong Ho. A slender, youthful woman, she talked shyly, with no display of emotion. Her four small children played around the room contentedly. With no hesitation, she informed me that the face on the picture marked by the X was that of Ah Wing, a business man of Honolulu. This surprised me, as Ah Wing's name had not shown up in the previous investigation.

Trying not to appear too eager, I asked:

"Was Ah Wing in business with Chin Shieu?"

Chong Ho answered in a low voice, gazing at the photograph as she spoke. Her husband had told her that Ah Wing was the boss of the smuggling organization which had brought into Honolulu the seized shipment of opium consigned to Chin Shieu's store. There were nine other men involved. Among them was her husband's father, Chin How, who lived in Macao, China.

I began to see that there was far more to this case than we had suspected.

Chong Ho talked on. Chin Shieu, she said, committed suicide because Ah Wing and the others in the Honolulu ring had deserted him after the contraband was seized.

"I not tell this to jury," she added, in her labored English. "Ah Wing get even."

Impassively, she said that when Ah Wing's syndicate was organized, he had promised all its members that they would be taken care of should any of them get into trouble. Legal fees would be paid and the families of members would be supported. But when Chin Shieu was arrested, Ah Wing had refused to help him, Chong Ho declared. Chin Shieu had been forced to pay his own legal expenses. His business had failed, his reputation was destroyed and, worst of all, his family honor had been blackened.

As I understand Chinese theology, there are three Chinese heavens. The lowest—number three—is a grim and awful place, like the hell of the Christian faith. A suicide must go to hell and suffer there throughout all eternity—unless he is avenged. But, let equal punishment fall on the enemy who had caused his death, and the tortured soul of Chin Shieu might rise to join his more fortunate ancestors. Obviously, Chin Shieu had marked the way for his avenger. The practical problem for a Customs man to solve then became: who loved Chin Shieu enough, and had power enough, to destroy Ah Wing?

Not Chong Ho. She was a woman, and the Chinese believed then that women do not share in matters pertaining to heaven and damnation. Not his children, either. They were too young.

But far away, in Macao, was Chin Shieu's father, Chin How. He had a motive—the affection of father for son, the strongest emotion known to a Chinese.

He also had the power. A word from him would be enough to convict Ah Wing of dope smuggling. Unfortunately, this would entail incriminating himself as well, breaking up a profitable business, and running the risks of an American jail—or a murderer's knife.

Besides, as far as I knew, Chin How was still in Macao and no one had told him of his son's manner of death. I could have written him a letter myself, but I had no assurance it would reach him, still less that he would believe a stranger.

So I composed a letter to headquarters in Washington, the gist of which was, "If you'll send me to Macao, I may be able to solve this thing."

They might have thought I was crazy. All I wanted to do was to go to Macao and persuade a wily old dope smuggler to give himself up voluntarily to justice five thousand miles away! Perhaps they thought that, being crazy, I was also expendable.

At any rate the answer came back:

"Go ahead."

Macao, a Portuguese colony about forty miles south of Hong Kong, has always been known as the international capital of dope smuggling. It is, therefore, no place for a U.S. Customs agent to stroll about carelessly. Before leaving Hawaii, I took some time to develop a new identity. I became John Holger, of New York, known in discreet circles as a buyer of opium. I boned up on the terms of the trade, studied the names of all the people connected with it, and practiced my few phrases of colloquial Chinese. I persuaded Chong Ho to give me the photograph marked with the X that had opened a new angle. As a possible method of introduction, I had myself photographed with Chong Ho and her four children. Then, half of a mind to burn candles to my own ancestors, I boarded the SS *President Johnson,* bound for Hong Kong.

The trip took twenty-three days. In Kowloon, on the mainland across the harbor from Hong Kong, I found rooms in a place that looked inconspicuous enough for my purposes. It was all of that. I picked up some shady acquaintances, hinted obliquely at powerful connections in the United States, and learned something of the cities of Kowloon and Hong Kong.

Several days later, I left for Macao on a small coastal steamer.

That unfortunate predecessor of the United Nations, the League of Nations, had ruled that only eleven chests of opium a year might be exported from India to Macao. Since the colony's chief source of income came from the transshipment of dope, nobody paid much attention to what the League of Nations said.

Besides the opium from India, almost the whole of south China's crop passed through Macao, minus League sanction. Large-scale gambling also kept the city's economic life prosperous. Macao's other name was the "Monte Carlo of the Far East."

But the principal industry of the town was the refining of opium, in a closely guarded factory known to smugglers all over the world as "The Farm".

In Macao I followed standard procedure to cover my tracks. I changed rickshas three times before going to the home of Chin How. This was a two-story mansion of an elaborate architectural style, located in the most fashionable part of town. Even among large houses, its size was remarkable. I learned later it had to be big. Chin How's family consisted of eight wives and uncounted children and servants.

To the doorman who opened to my knock I gave one of the photographs of Chong Ho and myself and said, in my best pidgin English, "You take me Chin How!"

He took the photograph and disappeared, returning in a few minutes to usher me into a large sitting-room. There stood a tall—over six feet—Chinese gentleman, with a wrinkled face, short white beard, a silk and obviously expensive gown, looking at me with scholarly benignity. Even without speaking a word, he was clearly a man of distinction, Chinese version. He motioned me to sit down, then sat down himself and clapped his hands. A procession of servants appeared, bringing food and drinks which were placed on low tables in front of us.

So far, no word had been spoken. Obviously he did not speak English. (Later I learned he knew a few English words, of which one was "Honolulu".)

My Chinese was of the practical sort used to direct ricksha drivers. So we ate and drank silently. Most of the foods were unknown to me. But the Chinese liquor he served was something I had tried before—samshui—which, literally translated, is "firewater". At the start I found everything delicious, but after an hour or two I became stuffed and uncomfortable. Yet there seemed no way out. Politeness required that he must continue to serve me. The same protocol demanded that I go on eating and drinking!

Over our chopsticks we would stare at each other. He would pull the photograph I had brought out of his sleeve and look at it affectionately, tapping the face of his son's wife with his long, well-shaped fingers, then tapping my shoulder as if to say, "You were a friend of my son's." Then he would pour more samshui and we would begin all over again. It was like a refined form of torture. Food seemed to be coming out of my ears. The liquor was anesthetizing my brain.

Then, suddenly Chin How got an inspiration. Seizing

my arm, he led me to an adjoining room where a Sun Life Insurance Company calendar decorated one wall. The old man pointed to the huge red sun which formed the principal ornament, and drew his finger five times around. Then he pointed to the Company's address in Hong Kong, and then to me.

I got his meaning. He wanted me to meet him at the Company's office in five days. I nodded in delight, circled the sun five times myself, and waddled out of his house, bloated as a pig.

Five days later I arrived at the offices of the insurance company. Chin How was waiting for me. The manager of the firm, Mr. Wong, greeted me in perfect English. He had been educated in the United States and had a precise diction which made my own speech sound rough and uncultured.

"You have, I am told, an important message for my friend".

I said that I had.

"Then I shall be pleased to interpret for you."

Mr. Wong's eyes opened wider as I told my story, but he interpreted it without comment. Chin How sat stiffly in his chair. If anything, he looked merely more dignified than before. When Wong had finished, he barked a few phrases and then, rising abruptly, stalked out of the room.

Mr. Wong turned to me. Distaste was plainly written on his face.

"Mr. Chin How says to tell you that you have made a great mistake. He is not in the narcotics trade. He never has been. He asks me to say goodbye for him and asks also that you do not bother him again. As for me, I am very busy this morning. If you do not mind—"

Suggestively, he held the door open. I walked out into the street, feeling a little sick.

"It's all in the game," I told myself. "You can't win every time."

Still, I felt none too good about facing the jeers of my fellow workers in Honolulu when I went back.

"Good old Hanks," they'd say. "Knows all about these Chinese customs!"

Just then I stopped feeling sorry for myself. Instinct told me I was being followed. Ducking into a narrow alley, I watched the man who was trailing me mince deliberately up the street. He was tall and patrician, with a white beard.

Chin How! For the first time since Mr. Wong had begun to translate my message, the old gentleman was smiling. I wondered what his motive was in following me. As I stopped, he took my arm and led me to the quay where the Macao boat docked. He pointed to the sun in the sky and made seven circles in the air, and then pointed to the boat. As the idea began to dawn on me, I couldn't help grinning. Apparently, Chin How did not trust Mr. Wong any more than I did. Anyway, he wanted to see me again.

Seven days later I went back to Macao, sought out Chin How's house again, and was admitted at once.

He had another guest at this time, a little old man named Sam Lee. Sam had run a store for years "on Mott Street in New York City." His American slang was dated. He had been away from our shores for many years. But Sam had come from the same village as Chin How, they had been friends since boyhood, and he was an interpreter the old man could trust.

So we settled down on comfortable chairs and the old fellow began, in mellifluous Chinese, a story that went on for hours. But when Sam Lee began to translate it into Mott Street English, I perked up my ears.

Mr. Wong, explained Sam Lee, was a highly respectable businessman who handled all of Chin How's legitimate investment, and the truth was not for his scrupulous ears.

The fact was that most of Chin's money, which was a lot, had been made from dope smuggling. He was, Sam Lee said proudly of his friend, a self-made man. Only two years before, he had organized an opium *hui*—Hawaiian word for company—with a capital investment of only $33,000. Profits to the *hui* for the first two years amounted to one million dollars, and this was cached in three different banks in Honolulu.

"What banks?"

But the old man was cagey. He didn't know the names of the banks. Nor the names of the depositors. For that matter, he did not know the name of the syndicate's treasurer. He was very, very vague about names.

Except Ah Wing's. When I showed Chin How the photograph with the X mark, his hands trembled and hate constricted his face. And when I suggested that he help bring Ah Wing to trial, he grinned with delight.

But he still didn't see any reason for giving away the names of the syndicate members. I had to begin a brief lecture on American justice. It would be expected, I said, that all the facts be brought out. We would have to prove a conspiracy. It all seemed like a lot of nonsense to him, but finally he agreed. Anything to make sure Ah Wing got the punishment he was due!

From a lacquered cabinet he brought out a mass of documents. Among them was a letter from Ah Wing, giving a complete profit and loss statement of the syndicate's operations. Unfortunately, it was written in Chinese and I would need someone to testify that it was in Ah Wing's handwriting. Chin admitted he could not read it himself. "But he has younger son in Honolulu—plenty smart—young fella, 'bout fifteen," Sam told me.

"Chin How send letter, tell young son to go court and tell judge ever'thing."

So far, so good. Now for the moment that would decide the success or failure of my mission. I turned to Sam Lee.

"Ask Chin How if he will return to Honolulu with me.

Ask him if he will go on the witness stand and testify on all that he has told me. Tell him clearly that if he does he will be indicted. He may have to stand trial and maybe go to jail. Of course I will do my best to see that he goes free as a government witness, and I believe I can succeed. But I'm not the judge. I can't make promises."

Then I sat back in my chair. I tried to look inscrutable. They jabbered in Chinese for a long time. Finally, Sam Lee said:

"He give you letter with all fact, and you give to judge. That be enough?"

"No. Tell Chin How that our laws do not permit evidence to be given that way. He must take the stand himself and let himself be cross-examined."

Neither man could understand this regulation. A barbarous practice of foreigners, apparently. Finally, Chin shrugged his shoulders.

"He do it!" cried Sam Lee.

I tried to keep the joy out of my face. Making some pious remarks about parental devotion, I exclaimed in all innocence:

"We can take the next ship for Hawaii!"

Both men flung up their hands in rejection. Chin How spoke swiftly in his native tongue. Sam Lee turned to me. "He can't go nex' boat."

"Why not?"

It took a long while to explain, Chinese fashion, and when I heard it in Sam's English, it still was not reassuring. Mr. Chin couldn't think of taking a sea journey without adequate spiritual preparation. He must, therefore, go back to his native village and worship the spirits of his ancestors. After that, he would go.

"How long will that take?"

"Two month," was the answer.

"But—"

The interpreter made a gesture of finality. "There is no way. He sail two month, that all."

There was nothing to do but go back to Honolulu alone.

I promised to reimburse Chin How for his expenses if he would follow me—though I knew that if the government refused to pay the claim, the money would come from my own pocket.

And I asked one last favor. "Let me see this Farm where the opium is refined."

Visiting the Farm was about as easy as getting admission to a nuclear research project today. Somehow Chin How arranged it. He visited a henchman of his, one Lim Lew. There was another reception, more food and drink, more palaver and procrastination. Finally, after three days of this, Lim Lew took me to the Farm.

The way there lay through the dirty crowded streets of downtown Macao. Our progress was accompanied by the chants of ricksha boys, the squeaking of ungreased wheels, the beating of drums (to keep devils away), and the whining of wretched beggars.

Suddenly I felt numb. Across a narrow alley about two hundred feet ahead but coming in my direction was Yung Go, a former resident of San Francisco's Chinatown. He knew me well as a Federal officer because I had assisted in his arrest for narcotic smuggling a few years before. He had served his sentence in McNeil Island Federal penitentiary and, upon his release, had been deported to his native China. If he saw me, my trip to China would have been useless, as he unquestionably would have found out my connection with Chin How.

My guardian angel must have been there. Yung Go turned into a doorway and disappeared without looking my way.

We came to a large godown which was surrounded by a heavy iron fence. Armed guards stopped us at the gate. In

answer to their gruff question, Lim Lew gave the right password. At the heavy teakwood door further on, Lim Lew repeated the password to two more guards. We went into an
enormous room, piled from floor to ceiling with five-tael cans
of opium.

The manager, Mr. Quon Lin, greeted us with proper
ceremony, as though he were the senior member of an exclusive club. Lim Lew, proud of his colloquial English, explained that I wanted to "give the place the once-over." I
was a "di gaw yen, a big-time smuggler." Quon Lin regarded
me with interest and apparent approval.

In his anteroom we drank tea and munched almond
cakes. While our nostrils drew in the rank smell of raw
opium, we discussed the weather. The two Chinese inquired
about the health and activities of their respective families,
speaking English for my benefit, in the courteous Oriental
fashion.

As the small talk continued, I began to despair of going
further, when at last Quon Lin asked me, "Do you really
care to inspect anything as insignificant as my factory?"

I shrugged my shoulders in pretended unconcern. "It
would not be too boring a way of passing an idle hour."

Ceremoniously, he led me through his establishment.
His long black robe trailed the floor. He pointed out the huge
vats in which the raw opium was boiled and treated until it
lay, brownish-black and gleaming, ready to be packed into
cans. Quon Lin kept shaking his head and uttering melan-
choly sounds. "In the old days, when the bulk of the raw
product came from India and Persia, we put out two high-
grade products, Lom Kee and Lom Kee Hop. But now," he
complained, "what with the League of Nations' ruling, we
are forced to mix cheap Yunnan opium with the fine stuff."

I noticed they had not changed the names of their
brands nor cut down their prices. It scarcely seemed tactful
to bring this up. "My friends in the United States had re-

marked on a deterioration of quality in recent years," I told him instead.

Quon Lin murmured something to himself.

A little later he asked me a touchy question. "What syndicate do you represent?"

I told him my syndicate did not want me to reveal its identity until I was ready to make a deal. I planned to visit similar establishments in other parts of China and in Persia. This turned out to be the right tactics. I gained considerable "face" by not giving away such vital information on such short acquaintance.

Quon Lin bowed politely. Lim Lew and I also bowed and left.

After I went back to Hong Kong, I took the next ship bound for Honolulu.

When I had written my report, I read it over. I had to admit that even to me it sounded a little insane. I was grateful that Sanford Wood, the U.S. attorney, didn't toss it in my face. But Wood had been around the Orient for a while. He read it, smiled and said, "Sure, sure, take it easy. We'll wait for Chin How."

But it was difficult to "take it easy." When I had left Chin How, I was convinced he meant every word he said. But now I began to wonder. Suppose he had been fooling me all the time? Or suppose his ancestors told him to forget about it? Or suppose some rival had done away with him?

After a long wait, on the fifth of June, I was informed that a ship had docked with a Chinese aboard who would speak only a name: "Mr. Hanks."

Down to the dock I sprinted and saw Chin How, tall and dignified as ever. I wanted to hug him. He looked at me gravely and explained, through an interpreter, that he was ready to do what I wanted.

We had already decided it would be necessary to hold Chin How incommunicado upon his arrival. This seemed extremely ungrateful to the old man. He could not see his younger son, nor his grandchildren. But we had to do it. We hid him away at the Immigration Service building and then tipped off the local papers. Headlines blazoned the news.

"Million Dollar Opium Case Reopened!"

"Macao Smuggler Makes Full Confession!"

Then we waited.

At midnight I received a telephone call. It was from Hong Suey, owner of a Chinese noodle house on School Street. He asked me to meet him at his restaurant.

There Hong Suey did the one thing I had never expected of a Chinese—he came straight to the point.

"You've really got Chin How here?"

"We have."

"I've been a gambler all my life," he said. "I'm used to taking chances. I've decided to plead guilty and turn state's evidence and throw myself on the mercy of the court."

Putting on my best poker face, I said, "This is a great surprise to me, Mr. Hong." And it was. Of all the names, Hong Suey's was one that Chin How never mentioned.

Hong made a gesture of negation.

"Don't try that on me, Mr. Hanks! I was the secretary-treasurer—and you know it. I have all the books. Wait—I'll show them to you here, now."

Before my incredulous eyes, he brought out several leather-bound books, kept in handsome Chinese script.

I got to the phone, routed the Collector of Customs out of bed, and requested:

"Send me a stenographer, please, right away."

The stenographer came, a tall, thin man, yawning behind his freckled hand. Hong Suey began methodically to translate. It took four hours to do—but it was worth a lifetime of sleuthing!

It was all there: how the syndicate had imported over 10,000 five-tael cans of opium (about six tons) in only two years; the names of the ships; the storage charges; the cost of operation; the gross and net profit, as well as the names of all the persons who had shared in it. This last was a great break for the income tax people, who were kept busy for years afterward filing suits on the basis of Hong's revelations.

It was five in the morning when I called Wilson Moore, assistant U.S. attorney who had been assigned by Wood to handle the case, and asked him to meet Hong at his office at nine o'clock.

Then, being half asleep, I made a mistake that almost proved disastrous.

Hong asked if he might keep the records until he went to Moore's office. It was only a few hours until then, and I was hardly able to keep awake. I said, "All right."

So when Hong showed up with the books, certain words and sections had been cut out with a razor blade.

"But why?" I moaned.

"To protect my small-fry customers who have done no wrong."

The mutilation, of course, practically ruined the evidence value of the books.

"What did you do with the pieces?"

"I burned them."

Wilson Moore banged his fist down on the table. "Then your books are useless to us, and you are useless as a government witness."

Hong Suey smiled then. "In that case, I admit I was lying."

He opened his shirt pocket and carefully brought out the missing fragments.

I drew a deep breath. Moore ordered Hong put into protective custody. The case of the government against the syndicate, the United States vs. Ah Wing et al., began to take shape.

Even so, we weren't out of the woods. The defense was wily, ingenious, never to be under-rated. The day before proceedings were to begin, a prominent Chinese gentleman came to my office to inform me that the interpreter had been paid $10,000 to misinterpret the testimony.

Anyone knows that an interpreter can make or break a case. We managed, though, to get another one appointed—just in time.

We got another jolt when Chin How's youthful scholar son took the witness stand. We had talked with Chin Lee. We knew he spoke perfect English. But on the stand he insisted he knew only Chinese. Every question had to be translated for him. Moore and I slumped in our chairs, certain that we had been double-crossed. But Chin Lee gave all the proper answers. When his testimony was finished and he emerged, plump and smiling, into the outer hall, I cornered him.

"Why no English on the stand, Chin Lee?"

He gave me an impish look. "I wished more time to think over my answers. While the translator talked, I thought. Has it not come out well?"

That he had perjured himself gave him no concern. That was a violation of our code, but not of his. This juxtaposition of the moral standards of East and West proved one of the most interesting things about the trial to me.

Old Chin How, who behaved throughout with the utmost composure, made it clear that what puzzled him most was the court's assumption that opium smuggling was something abhorrent. To him it was a legitimate as well as a profitable occupation.

With both Chin How and Hong Suey giving state's evidence, the defense had to resort to what we called "courtroom shenanigans." The defense counsel's plea to the jury was based chiefly on the fact that I was an outsider and had no business trying to tell Hawaiians how to live their lives.

We thought we had the case clinched, especially after Wilson Moore had cleverly maneuvered the defense counsel into demanding that the fragments cut from Hong Suey's books be produced, thereby being forced to accept them as valid evidence when the pieces were fitted into place.

But a few days before the trial—as we learned afterward—one of the jurymen, not a Chinese, sold a piece of property to one of the defendants for ten times its actual value.

The jury was irretrievably hung!

So, several months later we went through the new trial again. This time, the government won, hands down.

Ah Wing and his pals were sentenced to prison. Hong Suey got a suspended sentence. Chin How went free, with a handsome check to cover his travel expenses.

I went to see him, the day before he sailed, at Chong Ho's home. I found him covered with a quilt of grandchildren. Through his daughter-in-law, I expressed the Bureau's thanks for the sacrifices he had made. And my own thanks, as well.

Chin How loosened himself from small clutching hands and stood up. "It is I who owe you the thanks," he said, Chong Ho interpreting. "You journeyed to Macao at great risk to bring me news of the disgrace of my beloved son's soul. Through you I have been able to avenge his suicide."

A beatific expression came into his face. He gazed upward as though he could actually see Chin Shieu entering a heaven marked with a large Number One in Chinese characters.

And after I'd had a cermonial drink of samshui, I began to think I could see him, too!

I went back to San Francisco, glad to see the last of the Hawaiian smugglers. But in the work of Customs Agents, the same characters often appear again, either in major or minor roles.

Hong Suey gave me entree into one of the largest smuggling rings in the continental United States.

And that led directly to another case, known as *The Jade Tong Ring*.

The Jade Tong Ring

Part One

I HELD THE JADE RING in my hand. It was beautifully carved, with a heavy gold setting. Across the table, Chin Wah, who had given it to me, smiled his inscrutable Oriental smile.

"Put it on. It is yours. Not as reward but as warning—of what happen if you try double-cross!"

"Don't worry," I said, sliding the ring on my finger. I felt that by doing so I had settled my fate—Chin Wah had told me of the punishment reserved for those who turned traitor to the Tong—but I tried to answer his smile. Apparently, my reaction satisfied the Chinese, because he took a last swallow of tea and got up from the table.

"I have something for you about a week," he said. "Meet me usual place—it worth coming for!"

That was the beginning of my longest and most hazardous undercover adventure. For fourteen months I lived a dual existence—often challenging, always uncertain.

But it all was still ahead of me that day when, with the jade ring on my finger, I hurried back to the Customs office. I was eager to tell Supervising Agent Joe Green, Agent

Girard Polite, and Chief Inspector Roy Ballinger that I was "in".

This narcotics smuggling syndicate had been in existence for twenty years. Its headquarters was in Seattle and, at the time, was the largest ring in the United States. Distributing centers had also been set up in Chicago, Detroit and other large cities.

It was the dream and ambition of every Federal agent assigned to anti-narcotic smuggling matters to break this mob.

Therefore, when I was in Honolulu working on the Chin Shieu case, I was delighted to get a lead on this from Hong Suey. He had been secretary-treasurer of the Honolulu syndicate and had testified in behalf of the government.

Trying to stay in my good graces for reasons of his own, Hong Suey told me he had done business in the past with Chin Pak and Chin Wah, who he said were the bosses of the Seattle organization. He also said that they operated the American Oriental Taxicab Company in Seattle as a blind for their smuggling activities.

I realized that I was too well known as a Federal officer to attempt to make a big buy from the Seattle group. Even if I could I would not, merely through buying their stuff, find out about their smuggling methods.

So, after giving it much thought, I had Hong Suey write a letter of introduction for me to Chin Wah who, Hong Suey said, was the manager. I asked Hong Suey to make it plain that I was a Federal officer but, nevertheless, was a "good connection" and a good "friend" to have.

I knew that caution was necessary—that no entrapment methods be used that might later throw the case out of court. But getting to know personally the bosses of the organization might give me a break some time in the future.

The Customs Bureau in Washington was advised of my

plans in detail. Thomas J. Gorman, Deputy Commissioner of Customs, and Edson J. Shamhart, his chief assistant who handled the Criminal Investigation division of our department, wired their approval. (Later, Shamhart became Deputy Commissioner.)

Immediately following the completion of the Chin Shieu case in Honolulu, I went to Seattle. At the Oriental Taxicab Company office I presented my letter of introduction to Chin Wah.

His appearance conformed to the description Hong Suey had given me. His stocky figure seemed to be squeezed into a swivel chair behind the desk. As he rose to greet me I noticed he was of medium height. His square face had a determined expression which I later observed was habitual.

Smiling, he shook my hand courteously. Without giving my name I took the letter from my coat pocket and gave it to him.

"From your friend, Hong Suey," I said.

"You know him Honolulu?" Again Chin Wah smiled.

His face revealed nothing of his thoughts as he read the letter. It was written in Chinese and I never knew exactly how it was phrased. As Chin Wah deliberately folded it and slowly put it in his pocket, he appraised me closely.

Trying to seem casual, I told him I was to be stationed in Seattle. Still scrutinizing me intently, he finally spoke.

"You let me know when you get address."

That finished our first meeting. As I walked out the door, I hadn't the slightest idea of what Chin Wah thought of me.

A week later I called at his office again and gave him my address and telephone number.

Both the Collector of Customs men and the Customs Agents, the investigative group, believed that the Chin Wah smuggling contact was on the Blue Funnel Line of freighters. This line had British officers but large Chinese crews, and had regular runs between south China ports and Puget Sound cities.

This gave credence to our theory because Chinese like to do business with other Chinese rather than Caucasians. Also, the regular run feature of this particular shipping line would permit fixed, definite arrangements for the smuggling plans.

With a representative of both the Customs Agency and the Collector's office, I called on the commanding officer of the Coast Guard in the Seattle area, Captain R. W. Dempwolf. We explained our suspicions and plans. Captain Dempwolf was very interested and cooperative. He said that even though his command was then short of vessels, he would do his best to have any suspect ship followed while in American waters, as well as watched while docked.

He asked that we notify the Coast Guard when any suspect vessel was due, so that he could help with our plan.

Later, when I began to request that all Blue Funnel Line freighters be followed and watched, the Coast Guard maintained continuous vigil.

Approximately six weeks after this procedure was started, I received a telephone call from Chin Wah, asking me to call at his office. When I arrived there he extended a personal invatation to a large Chinese dinner to be given in a private room at a nearby restaurant.

At the dinner, Chin Wah discussed Honolulu, politics and almost everything else before finally showing his true reason for inviting me.

In the large convivial crowd, I looked as closely as possible, without being conspicuous, to see if I recognized anyone, but there was no one I was able to identify.

"How you like assignment in Seattle?" he inquired.

This gave me the opportunity I was waiting for. I told

him that at my request we were now concentrating on the Blue Funnel Line ships and would continue to do so. From his reaction to this statement, I hoped to find out whether he was using these ships for his smuggling. Also, I wanted Chin Wah to know that I was largely responsible for this increased vigilance, and that I was the one he would have to deal with if he wanted this surveillance stopped.

Chin Wah, the Oriental, kept a poker face. So I could not tell whether this bit of information interested him or not.

We continued, however, to request a Coast Guard trail on all the Blue Funnel ships. Six weeks went by before I heard again from Chin Wah.

He wanted me to meet him for lunch at an oyster house in Chinatown.

In a private booth at the restaurant, we talked about various inconsequential subjects before Chin Wah finally came to the point. He said he had a friend who was interested in our following the Blue Funnel Line ships so constantly. This friend, he added, had come to him wanting to know if anything could be done about it. He, himself, Chin Wah declared, had no particular interest in the matter, but was merely passing on his friend's remarks.

As long as I was not asked a direct question, I parried the subject, fearing all the time, however, that my face betrayed the triumph I felt.

As we were ready to leave the place, Chin Wah asked, "What shall I tell my friend?"

It was out at last. Trying not to muff my advantage, I managed to say I would think it over and let him know in a day or two.

Upon returning to my office I immediately consulted with the Supervising Customs Agent and Captain Dempwolf. We contacted our Washington headquarters, explained the situation, and were told to go ahead with our plan. We also saw the U.S. attorney in Seattle and advised him of our strategy, which he approved.

Since eagerness is contemptible in Chinese eyes, I waited two days before calling Chin Wah. Then I arranged for a meeting later. At that time I told him that the following of a particular freighter could be called off at specific times, but I would have to be advised in advance the name of the ship. Furthermore, I would have to receive quite a sum of money first, I added.

Chin Wah, showing no surprise, replied that he would tell his friend and would call me when he had a message from him. He said, however, that we should use caution in our telephone conversations and not mention names or places. "Bellingham" was the identifying word we were to use to each other on the telephone, Chin Wah said, so as to be certain we were not talking to someone else.

After the word "Bellingham", he continued, there was to be no further conversation except this: "Number One", which meant that we were to meet right away near the corner of Seventeenth and Jefferson streets; "Number Two" meant another prearranged place; and "Number Three" still a third designated corner. One of us would get into the other's car and then we would do our talking while driving around.

On the night before the next Blue Funnel freighter was due in Seattle, I answered the phone at my home. I could tell at once it was Chin Wah, but waited for the word "Bellingham". When it came, I answered identically. "Number One", the voice directed.

I drove at once to the intersection of Seventeenth and Jefferson and picked up Chin Wah. As soon as he got in he handed me two hundred dollars and said:

"My friend says don't follow the ship tomorrow night when it goes to Everett."

I had to put on an air of dissatisfaction with the amount of money received.

"Chin Wah, I won't go for such chicken feed next time," I complained.

He said that was all the friend could afford just then.

"You get more jobs soon—more money, too," he added, in a placating tone.

As soon as I could get to the office, I advised the Supervising Agent, the U.S. attorney, and Captain Dempwolf of my meeting with Chin Wah. We noted the serial numbers on the bills he had given me and the money was placed in the vault in the office of the Collector of Customs. We also arranged not to have that particular freighter trailed.

Two weeks later I received again the "Bellingham" signal over the telephone from Chin Wah. Again it was "Number One".

Upon meeting him I could tell he was in a car I had never seen before. This time he picked me up. He gave me a set of keys and said, "Some time when I call you and you come and I not here but car is, you open back end. Then you find direction what to do."

About a week after this, in answer to such a summons, I saw the same car parked, but no one in it. I found the right key to open the trunk. Inside was a large package with printed instructions to put the unopened package in a pay locker at the bus depot. I was also directed to leave the key to the locker in the car, park it where I found it, and return home.

I felt this to be a "dry" trial run to test whether I would open the package or take it to the Customs office. Actually, I was tempted to do just that, but I realized that if it were a parcel of narcotics, about the only person I could arrest would be myself because so far we had no valid proof against Chin Wah. So I carried out the instructions carefully. Also in the trunk was a hundred dollars in bills. This

went into the Customs safe with the other money, in an envelope signed by witnesses.

Subsequently, I delivered other packages. Again, the
money and memoranda each time went into the Customs
safe. The file on Chin Wah and Chin Pak began to grow. But
at all our conferences and telephone calls to Washington, it
was decided not to make any arrests or seizures as yet.

Now that I had made several deliveries, we thought we
might get somewhere. We were up against the problem of
evidence. More corroboration, more supporting facts were
needed.

My business meetings with Chin Wah had always taken
place in cars, usually mine. So we decided that the next
meeting between the smuggling boss and myself in my car
would be covered by Agent Girard Polite. He would hide in
the rear compartment of my coupe and listen to our conversation.

In the privacy of my garage, we practiced—first, to see
if Polite could hear a normal tone of voice from the trunk;
then to determine whether there was any noticeable move-
ment if Girard changed his position. It was necessary that
Polite actually see Chin Wah so he could testify later in
court that he saw and heard this particular individual.

In order to make sure of this, we drilled holes in the
rear compartment on the right side. In practicing, however,
we found that, in looking out through the hole, Polite had to
lie on his side. Then, in order to be even partly comfortable,
he had to turn on his back. When he rolled over, the car
shook noticeably. So we decided that, just as Chin Wah
stepped into the car, Polite at that moment was to roll over.

Polite had to live at my house until the next call came
from Chin Wah. In the early morning, a few days after
Girard had taken up residence with me, the phone rang. When
I answered I heard the familiar "Bellingham—Number One",
to which I responded as directed.

Polite and I went to the car. I did not envy his role. He

took a last puff at his cigarette, tossed away the butt, and
vaulted into the rear compartment. I watched while he
wound up in a blanket and wriggled down into the least uncomfortable position possible on the floor.

"If I feel like coughing, I'll have to gag myself," Polite
said with a grin as I closed the cover, and locked it. Then I
hung the key on the garage wall. I then would not be able to
open the compartment, no matter how suspicious Chin Wah
might become.

At Seventeenth and Jefferson, I parked the coupe and
stuck my head out the window. All of Seattle seemed full
that early dawn with Oriental eyes. My jade ring reflected a
momentary beam of light. Then I saw Chin Wah.

"Here he comes, Girard", I almost whispered. "Take a
look!"

Chin Wah, dressed in expensive gabardine and a pearl
grey hat, casually opened the door of the car and stepped in.
As he did so I could sense that Girard was turning over, but
the Chinese slammed the door so hard that Polite's move-
ment was not noticeable.

"Drive around the block," ordered Chin Wah.

I did—keeping a close watch through the rear window
to be sure we were not being followed. But evidently, all the
worry was not on my side of the fence. When, at his command, I parked again and shut off the motor, he shook his
head.

"Start engine again. Keep running so nobody hear us."

Now I really was in a spot. And Polite in a far worse
one. With the motor running it would be only a matter of
minutes before the fumes would overcome him.

"Let's roll up the windows instead," I said. Leaning
past Chin Wah I cranked up the window on his side, then did
the same with mine. This seemed to satisfy the Oriental.

I could almost hear Girard's sigh of relief!

"Well, what's the assignment this time, Chin Wah?"
His answer bowled me over.

"I promise you real chance, when I give you ring. Now, you like take some junk Chicago?"

This might be my chance to learn the contacts in the Midwest—perhaps to crack the whole nation-wide ring.

Forcing myself to appear indifferent, I grumbled, "How much is in it for me?"

"Plenty. Five hundred and expenses."

I laughed scornfully. "I thought we were through with the small change. I won't go for anything less than a thousand."

"No, Chin Pak say five hundred. Take it or leave."

At last Chin Wah had named Chin Pak. Since Hong Suey had told me he was the boss of the syndicate, I had been waiting to hear Chin Wah mention his so-called "friend"—actually his boss—by name. Outwardly, Chin Pak was a respectable citizen of Seattle, and a prominent member of the Chin family Tong.

I figured that both Chin Pak and Chin Wah would have more faith in me if I bickered a little about my pay. As a preparation for a bout of haggling, we both lit cigarettes simultaneously. As we did so, as if in answer to a signal, we saw a shadowy figure approach. Sure that Chin had set a trap for me, I put my hand on my gun holster. Chin Wah, suspicious as always, apparently thought the same thing of me, for his hand reached toward his gun and he leaned forward, tensely. Then the man, standing not four feet from us, stopped to light his pipe. At once, we both recognized him as the custodian of the city playground near which we were parked.

Chin Wah and I looked at each other, smiled with mingled relief and embarrassment, and replaced our weapons.

At that time I could easily have reached a compromise with Chin Wah. But I wanted another meeting, more corroboration of his complicity. So I refused to come down a cent —and demanded an interview with Chin Pak.

Finally, Chin Wah said he would arrange it for the next evening. Same time and place. Then he left the car and walked away jauntily.

Next day there was a squabble at the Customs office. Supervising Agent Green wanted to occupy the car trunk. Polite insisted he had a priority. Finally, Green pulled his rank and gave himself the assignment.

Everything went smoothly that night. Chin Wah and I again sat in my car—Green listening in the compartment—and resumed our haggling.

"You promised to let me talk to Chin Pak tonight," I argued.

"You drive his house, one hour after I leave you. Garage door already open. You drive in," directed Chin Wah.

After he left, I took Green back to the office. He had heard the entire conversation and would be able to testify as to every detail discussed. We joyfully recounted the evidence that we felt no defense counsel could impugn.

It was exactly one hour after Chin Wah got out of my coupe that I drove through the open door of Chin Pak's garage. Chin Wah ushered me through a door at the side of the garage directly into a spacious, well-lighted room. Heavy silk draperies covered the windows and several large embroidered Oriental pictures hung on the walls.

Chin Pak acknowledged my introduction with a handshake. Older than Chin Wah, he stood several inches taller. His black hair was cropped short and his eyes had a serious, but alert expression.

Unsmiling, he said to me, "Glad you with us."

"I'm pleased to work for you and also to talk to you," I replied.

The three of us sat down on elaborately-carved Oriental chairs, and I waited for Chin Wah to speak, but he evidently was remaining silent in deference to his superior.

Boldly, I said:

"I must have more money to go to Chicago. The risk is worth all of a thousand."

Chin Pak shook his head. "No, too much", he repeated.

He offered me $700 and expenses. Feeling that I had bargained successfully in getting a higher offer than the first, I accepted it.

As I rose to go, Chin Pak pointed to the jade ring on my finger, then to the one he was wearing. He and Chin Wah both impressed on my mind the honors and penalties that the wearing of the ring involved.

Part Two

For days I was so busy lining up details that I would forget any possible danger. But whenever I took off the ring and set it on the sink while I washed my hands, it always reminded me of the possible consequences of the double-cross.

After several conferences and telephone calls to Washington, it was decided that Girard Polite would make the trip to Chicago with me. We would take adjoining rooms and he would have charge of the telephone recorder device and the dictaphone. We would ride the same Great Northern train since dapper Chin Wah, who was to be the group's contact man, was traveling by the Northern Pacific railroad.

The trip was scheduled to start January 27, 1935. On the evening of the 26th, I drove to Chin Pak's. As I started to park at the curb before his house, he came out and told me to drive into the garage.

I had a bad moment when he fingered the peep hole in the trunk, but I was able to explain it away.

"Bad aim," said Chin Pak. "You come in and have drink."

In the house he handed me a slip of paper. "You call Chin Wah this number—noon—day you get Chicago. He take charge then."

I was more nervous than an expectant father. Every

second I thought Chin Pak would startle me with some question for which I might lack a plausible answer. Finally, he went to the window, looked out and nodded to someone outside. Then he said to me:

"It o.k. you leave now. You find sacks of stuff in your car. Good luck!"

He held out his hand. As I shook it, his jade tong ring touched my palm.

With a forced smile I said, "Be seeing you!" And I got out of there quickly.

Ballinger and Polite were waiting in my garage. We hauled two gunny sacks out of the rear compartment. Inside each sack were four packages wrapped in heavy brown paper. Each contained ten five-tael cans of opium.

"We'd better take a sample," Ballinger suggested," So we can prove the cans contained hop when we get into court."

I looked around for a playing card. Polite punched a hole in one of the cans with a nail, dug some of the gummy, black opium out, and dropped a little on the card. Then we put the card and opium into an envelope, sealed it, initialed it, and marked the date on the outside.

"We'll have to seal that can again," I said. "Of course they'll get suspicious if they notice that hole."

"Right," said Ballinger. "Got a soldering iron?"

"Yes, an electrical one."

I got it out and connected it. The idea was excellent. The only trouble was that it didn't work. Every time the hot iron touched the can, opium swelled and oozed out.

We kept trying. Time was passing. Long after midnight, each of us bathed in sweat, we gave it up as a bad job. Still, we had to close that can, and it must be done before the train left—at 7 a.m.!

"I'll get some liquid solder," Polite volunteered. "They're sure to have it at any drug store."

"What drug store?" asked Ballinger. "Do you realize it's 3 a.m.?"

"Oh, I'll find one that's open all night." Polite was the optimistic sort. He hurried out and we heard him starting his car.

It was near daylight when he returned. He brought with him not only the solder but a weird assortment of glue, paste, sealing wax and paraffin.

Working at breakneck speed, we put a piece of paraffin over the hole, hardened it in the refrigerator, then pasted a piece of wrapper from another can over it. It looked perfect. Later, when I eventually delivered the can in Detroit, it passed muster without question.

It was now six in the morning. We said goodbye. Polite was to board the train later at Everett, so that none of Chin Pak's spies might see him at the Seattle station. Ballinger's hand-grip seemed more intense than the occasion warranted, but as I felt the ring press into my skin, I understood.

After they left I packed the cans in the bottom of my trunk, threw my clothes in on top and was just locking it when the expressman rang the doorbell. He grumbled at the weight, asking if I were a brick salesman carrying a load of samples.

I gulped a cup of coffee, kissed my wife and little girl, and got into a taxi. Then I was on the train and the porter was calling breakfast. But somehow I had no appetite.

Two days later, during the stopover at St. Paul, the train began to jerk and bang. It was after ten at night, but Girard and I were still in the club car, re-rehearsing our plans.

"What's wrong?" I asked, as the porter was thrown against me by a sudden lurch.

"The Northern Pacific sleeping cars," he told us, regaining his balance. "We carry them for the rest of the trip, sir."

I bounced to my feet. The Northern Pacific! And Chin Wah was in one of those coaches! Suppose he should come forward to visit me? And so see Girard? That would be the finish of the trip, right there in St. Paul. He had seen Polite before. He even pointed him out to me once. There wasn't a chance he would not recognize him.

Polite wanted to hop off the train and take the next one. I was afraid, however, that Chin Wah might see him when he crossed the lighted platform, so he decided to get into his berth and keep the curtains closed. Then, before dawn, he could sneak off at some way station.

He did just that—but a true story like this is full of anti-climaxes, of many build-ups and tensions that fade into nothing. This was one. Chin Wah stayed in his own car. Later, he told me he had slept so soundly he had not heard his car being switched over to our train. So Polite would not have had to sneak off at Aurora, about thirty miles out of Chicago, and drive the rest of the way in a taxi.

In Chicago I went to the Morrison Hotel. There I insisted on seeing the manager. I explained I was with the Customs Service and needed two adjoining rooms, but that no one should know that Polite and I were together nor who we were. He was very cooperative. The rooms he selected even had a connecting door, to which each of us was given a key.

Girard arrived an hour later. As soon as the porter brought up his trunk, we unpacked the dictaphone and recording instrument. At first we were lucky. The telephone was on the wall between the rooms, so we could shove the tapped wires through the hole we punched inconspicuously in the wall of Polite's room. The microphone was hooked to a lampshade over my dresser and the wires ran along the electric light wires into his room. Then, our task done, we tested it. . . . and it did not work!

Painstakingly we went over each connection. We took as much of the set apart as we dared, to see if anything had been broken in transit. We put it together again. Once more we tested it. Still it was as dead as ever.

Then we discovered the trouble. The set was made for alternating current—Chicago's Loop was on direct current.

It was now eleven o'clock. At noon I was to call Chin Wah. We desperately wanted a record of that conversation, to show it had been pre-arranged, as a tie-in with those we had logged in the car. So Polite dashed out of the hotel with a list of nearby electrical appliance shops hurriedly taken from the telephone directory.

While he was gone, I called Fred Gardner of the Chicago Customs office from a booth in the downstairs drugstore. (Later Gardner became Supervising Agent at San Francisco.) Joe Green had guaranteed him as a man who could be trusted absolutely. He was the sole Agent I contacted in Chicago. He promised cooperation and he made good his promise.

He and Girard arrived at the same time. Polite had found an apparatus to make the necessary change of current. We attached it, found the machine worked perfectly, and were ready for the telephone call.

With my blood pressure several points higher, I called the number Chin Pak had given me. Chin Wah answered.

"Meet me," he said, "at the Clark Street entrance of the hotel at seven tonight."

The conversation was duly recorded.

We arranged for Polite to stay in his room and log all interviews and phone calls, while Garner was to shadow me whenever I left the hotel.

That evening Chin Wah picked me up and drove me to a small apartment hotel on Dorchester Avenue. He introduced me to the owner, another well-educated Chinese named Chin Gooi who, I learned, was their principal Chicago contact.

Over whisky sours, they made arrangements for the Chins and myself to take twenty of my cans to Detroit as soon as the consignees wired that the money was on hand to pay for them. There are no charge accounts in the narcotics racket!

They drove me back to the Morrison in Chin Gooi's car. It was an easy matter to memorize the license number, but unnecessary. I invited them up for drinks but they declined. As they drove away, I saw that Gardner's car was not far behind.

Part Three

The next day we began making deliveries. This was hardly more exciting than if we had been delivering milk. Nor much more dangerous, apparently. You put the requisite number of cans in your briefcase, you were driven to the agreed place of transfer (usually a Chinese-owned restaurant), you put your briefcase on the floor beneath the table. When you were ready to leave you picked it up and found it empty. Then you went back to the hotel. As routine as delivering milk, but not half as healthy. Instead of fresh air, you breathed oxygen permeated with the smells of frying onions and decaying garbage. It was neither thrilling nor romantic. Just plain boring.

Only once, on the whole trip, did a delivery have a touch of adventure. In obedience to a phone call from Chin Wah, I had met him on the corner outside the hotel with ten cans of opium in my usual briefcase issued to me by the Treasury Department. Chin Gooi was driving. He, Chin Wah and another Oriental, who I guessed was one of their bodyguards, were in the car. I got in the front seat and we drove to Michigan Boulevard, then headed right. As a red light forced us to stop, a red Buick with a man driving and a woman in the front seat halted in the next traffic lane simultaneously. They glanced at us, carelessly at first, then their gaze became a scrutiny.

Something about the way the man stared—the quick but careful look of appraisal—told me he must be a law enforcement officer. He had reason for suspicion. In Seattle or San Francisco, there would have been nothing unusual about three Chinese and one American white man riding in a car together. But in Chicago it was not ordinary.

Then the traffic light changed. We speeded ahead, but there was another stop light at the next intersection. Again the two cars stopped side by side. Once more we were expertly scrutinized. My spine tingled. If I were in the other car, I would force ours to the curb—make a rapid search—find the opium in the briefcase—and arrest all four of us.

Eventually, Gardner would help clear my reputation—but my trip would come to a sudden and disastrous end. Chin Wah would believe it was a put-up job, that I had tricked him. At that time, Chinese hatchet men could be hired cheaply in Chicago. Chin Wah, I felt, would consider the price of my demise an investment and not an expense.

Again at the third traffic light the two cars drew up parallel. I saw the man say something to his companion, who spoke swiftly in answer.

"This is it," I told myself.

Chin Wah, also watching the red Buick, now became very agitated, speaking rapidly in Chinese to our other passengers. He barked at me in English, "Get gun—get gun!" A quick glance told me he was holding on to his own gun underneath his overcoat.

I obeyed him and got my gun ready, though I had no intention of using it on the man in the Buick.

But nothing happened. Perhaps the wife said, "Please, not now—we're late already for church!" Perhaps the man thought of the likelihood of gun play and her safety and decided not to risk it on that possible chance. As the light turned green, the Buick drove ahead, we turned right and saw it no more.

When I told Gardner about it later, he identified the license number as that of a Federal narcotics agent's car.

We stopped before a Chinese restaurant, entered and ordered a meal.

While we were eating, a strange Chinese, carrying a suitcase, came in, glanced around, then walked confidently up and sat down at our table. As usual, I concentrated on memorizing his features and marks of identification so that, when the blowoff came, it would be easy to recognize him.

In this case, it was hard to do. He was dark-skinned, smoothly shaven, apparently middle-aged and clearly prosperous. There was nothing to distinguish him from many others of his race. That is, until he smiled—revealing a prominent gold tooth!

"You bring stuff?"

Chin Wah nodded. Gold Tooth produced a roll of bills and handed them over. Chin stooped, picked up my briefcase and gave it to Gold Tooth, who started toward the door.

"Hey!" I said to Chin Wah. "What's he doing?"

My briefcase had never been taken away before, and had remained in my presence during previous deliveries.

I could feel drops of sweat on my forehead. It had suddenly flashed on me that the briefcase the other Chinese was carrying away had the words "U.S. Government" plainly stamped on the inside lining.

But Chin Wah said unconcernedly, "He'll bring back."

I drank some tea. It was scalding hot and almost parboiled my throat, distracting me for a moment. By the time I had cooled off, Gold Tooth returned with the briefcase. I held my breath, waiting for him to comment on the lettering. But he only smiled, nodded and ordered egg foo yung. Later, when I looked into the case, I saw that he had taken the cans out without disturbing the wrapping paper. And the paper had hidden the government stamp.

That was the last of our Chicago deliveries.

Next day Chin Wah told me: "Tomorrow you take morning train Detroit. Chin Gooi and I go by car. We meet you this address." He handed me a paper that looked like a Chinese laundry list with a heading in both languages.

I suppressed a smile. For ways that are devious and tricks that deceive, the Chinese are world masters. The reason for their going by auto was, of course, to leave me holding the bag. If I were arrested they would have a perfect alibi—they had gone to Detroit merely to attend a Chin family get-together.

Gardner went with me to Detroit, to keep up with the contacts I made. We left Girard Polite behind to give him a chance to see that Chicago consisted of more than one single hotel room.

After I met Chin Wah and Chin Gooi at the Detroit laundry, we went to another Chinese restaurant. By now I was getting very tired of noodles and sweet-and-sour spareribs. There I made my first Detroit delivery, including the can that had been tapped and sealed in my garage. Luckily, it passed unnoticed.

Two days later we were finished. Chin Wah told me to get packed. He and I were driving back to Chicago with Chin Gooi. They would pay me off on the road.

This was a set-back. My plans called for payment in Chicago—in the hotel room—where it could be recorded for use in court. I also had to warn Gardner to get back to Chicago quickly. While packing my bags I talked to him, promising that I'd stall on the trip as much as I could so that he could arrive in the Windy City first.

En route, Chin tried to make payment of the $700 on which we had agreed in Seattle. I shook my head. "I won't take a chance on being stuck up by Chicago gangsters. I'll wait—you can pay me when we get to the hotel."

He shrugged. "Well, o.k. But no danger here. We got our guns."

Chin Gooi left us at the hotel entrance in Chicago. He

had planned a big party later that evening. Chin Wah and I started for the elevator. All the way up in the elevator and down the hall to my room I worried. Suppose Gardner's train was late? Suppose the machines had gone haywire, or that Polite had not yet returned to the room?

This was the payoff, the moment for which we had worked so long. If we didn't put it over. . . .

There was no use surmising. There was nothing to do but put my key in the lock and open the door.

The room was empty. But Chin Wah intended to make certain. He looked under the bed, opened the closet door, and then he gave me a terrific scare. Walking to the door between my room and Polite's, he grasped the knob and shook it violently, then he pounded two or three times on one of its panels.

I had told Girard and Fred that if I needed help I would knock three times on this connecting door. They were to rush in then, ready for action. Now I expected calamity! Loudly, I said:

"That door's been locked ever since I moved in, Chin Wah. There's no use your trying it."

I waited. Apparently they had been listening on the dictaphone and knew the knocks were tests and not signals. Or weren't they there?

A moment later Chin Wah gave me still another fright. He was very vain and never overlooked a chance to admire himself. Now he walked to the dresser, took out a pocket comb and began grooming his hair. The dictaphone mike was concealed in the light shade immediately above his head. If he leaned forward, he had only to glance up to see it!

But luck still held. Chin smirked approvingly at his reflection without looking upward, then put the comb away. Going into the bathroom, he brought out two glasses, took a pint of excellent whisky from his pocket and poured us each a drink.

We started to talk. I wanted to bring the conversation

around to some of the opium dealings, so it would be plain to a jury later just what we were talking about.

"You certainly made all the deliveries here very slick!" Chin Wah beamed. He had a weakness for flattery.

"I was afraid only once," I went on, "and that was when you had me take the three cans of opium to that strange Chinaman late in the evening."

"You no should be 'fraid. I in charge," he boasted.

For half an hour we talked over some of our past dealings. The entire history of the case went down on the records in Chin Wah's own voice.

At last he paid me off, counting out the bills as he handed them to me. Then we left together to attend the victory dinner.

As we walked down the hall I saw Gardner waiting at the elevator. At the trial he would now be able to identify Chin Wah positively as having been the person in the room with me.

I got back from the party as soon as I could.

"How did it go?" I shouted to Polite.

"Perfect. We got every word. Listen!"

As he played back the recordings, I heard every part of my conversation with Chin Wah.

The case seemed to be clinched. So next day, Girard and I returned to the West Coast.

Back in Seattle, we played the records over again in the office. I turned in the descriptions of Chin Gooi and every other contact I had made in Chicago and Detroit.

We agreed we had sufficient evidence to win our case. But there was one more obstacle—we still did not know how the actual smuggling was accomplished. If we ended our case now, we might never find out how the dope was brought in. Someone else might continue to use that successful method.

However, luck came our way again. Two days after our return to Seattle I met Chin Wah by appointment. He seemed excited. One of his men, he said, had been killed on a speedboat by hijackers.

"You take his place. I promote you," he added blandly, waving his hand in a benign gesture.

This unwelcome "promotion" tempered my inner excitement at the prospect of finding out what we were so anxious to know. This was the first time I had heard of any speedboat being owned or operated by the Chin Pak outfit.

Trying to appear unimpressed, I said: "All right. What do I do?"

He told me where to find the boat. I was to go aboard after dark that night; I would find three other men already there who would be expecting me. But first, I was to arrange it so no Coast Guard cutter would be following the Blue Funnel freighter that would shift from Seattle to Everett that night.

I followed the directions after first notifying the Supervising Agent and the Coast Guard of the plans.

About 10 p.m. I went to a cove where the speedboat was moored close to shore. There was enough light for me to see my associates distinctly. All three were white men whom, to my knowledge, I had never seen before. They glanced at me but said nothing. As we waited there was no talking. Finally about midnight I saw a large steamer coming down the Sound. Our speedboat got underway and maneuvered so as to be in a position about a quarter of a mile away when she passed us.

As the big vessel came abreast, one of the men in our boat flashed a light three times. From one of the portholes three flashes answered him. I expected some kind of immediate action, but nothing apparently happened. We drifted silently for an hour or more, still with no conversation.

At about 1:30 a.m. the helmsman got our boat started. When we reached the area through which the steamer had passed I could see a light bobbing with the waves. As we came close, I saw that it was a flashlight turned on inside a milk bottle which had been well sealed. The bottle and flashlight were connected to a long string of thirteen cylindrical packages or long "sausages", so shaped as to go through a round porthole. All the packages were attached to large, cork floats.

As we pulled the packages aboard, I could tell that one of them, now limp, and almost empty, had contained salt. We opened the others. All twelve contained an immense quantity of morphine, heroin and opium.

We made a landing on an isolated spot on the beach where a small truck was waiting to receive the contraband. One of the men in the boat stayed to drive the truck. The rest of us then returned in the boat to our point of departure.

There I was spoken to for the first time. "Go home—nowhere else," the helmsman ordered.

Next morning I eagerly reported all details to my brother officers. We all were curious about the package of salt. After experimenting, we finally found that the salt was heavy enough to take the entire shipment under water and hold it there for a period of an hour. By that time enough salt had been dissolved to allow the floaters to bring the entire shipment to the surface. There the bobbing flashlight would guide the smugglers to their contraband.

We were overjoyed that at last we knew how this gang conducted their smuggling. But we wondered why, under the circumstances, Chin Wah was so fearful of the Coast Guard's trailing. Later, when he paid me for the night's work, with Polite again listening from the car trunk, Chin Wah voluntarily admitted that he was afraid the salt sack might at some time come loose from the "sausages". This would allow the stuff to remain on the surface as soon as it was dropped, and thus be found at once by the Coast Guard ship following closely behind the freighter. He also feared hijackers.

At the Customs office we held a long conference. We decided we had everything we needed now except one more thing. We must seize some contraband to end the case. It was further decided to do this at the pier, if possible, to give us more witnesses and to have more defendants.

How was this to be accomplished? To make the gang change their system would require some fast talking. My chance to do this came a week later when, in the midst of a terrific storm on the Sound, the next Blue Funnel freighter was reported due. On this trip she was to unload in Seattle and then return to the Orient without making any other port. The dope must be unloaded there or it would have to go back to China.

I called Chin Wah and met him at Number One. I told him I was sure it would be impossible to transfer the dope anywhere except at the pier. I knew a Customs man, I said, who was open for a "take." For $500 he would see that no one interfered. There was a lot of argument and Chin cut the imaginary traitor down to $350, but I won the point.

The smugglers planned to have their speedboat stand by about half a mile from the freighter docked at the pier. They would send a rowboat in from the speedboat to go under the stern portholes of the freighter. At the same time, the Number One Boy on the ship would lower the stuff to the rowboat. Then the rowboat would take the contraband out to the smugglers' waiting speedboat.

I hastened back to contact Green and Polite.

We were coming to the end of the trail. After much discussion, we made our plans:

Customs Agents in two rowboats would start working their way along under the piers as soon as it was dark enough to get to the vessel unnoticed. Without being seen, the *Arcata,* one of the larger Coast Guard ships, could be stationed approximately a mile away on the far side of the distant speedboat in which Chin Wah's underlings expected to haul away the loot. The Coast Guard ship *Zev,* a captured rum runner, would be brought in close to the dock after dark, ready for pursuit.

When I heard the first load being moved into the rowboat, I was to fire a Very pistol loaded with a star shell, from the pier.

Then Chin Wah tossed all our plans into a cocked hat. He phoned and said briskly, "No will do."

"Why not?" I was aggrieved and showed it. "I've made all arrangements. If you can't do it tonight the stuff can go back."

Chin Wah suggested that I come to Chin Pak's house and talk it over.

The men in our office looked at me soberly. "Don't give up," I told them, feigning a confidence I didn't feel. "They might still change their minds. Be ready, just in case—"

I arrived at Chin Pak's house about seven o'clock. Chin Pak and Chin Wah argued and stalled until almost nine. Then Chin Pak made his decision:

"Go right now."

I knew then that he had begun to distrust me—that he had been afraid to give me a chance to tip anyone off. It was just as well that our dealings were coming to a climax.

We drove to the pier where the freighter was berthed. While Chin Pak and Chin Wah stayed in the car, I walked down the dock. I dismissed the two guards on duty, telling them to be sure to show themselves as they left, and to go to the Great Northern dock, which was the next pier.

Then the wait began.

I had time, standing there in the darkness, to doubt the wisdom of every plan I had made. I wondered about the

Very pistol. If I fired it at the wrong moment there would not be another chance. The first shell would warn the smugglers that I had betrayed them.

Then there came a flash of light from the inside stern porthole—answered by a wink from the dark waters of the Sound. The smugglers' speedboat had established contact.

Several minutes later, I heard the bump of the rowboat against the big ship. From the place where I stood I could not see the skiff.

Allowing a moment for the stuff to be lowered, I wondered if the guards were ready and if the other Agents were hidden in their rowboat under the pier, as they had planned.

I pointed the Very pistol into the air and squeezed the trigger.

There was noise and a burst of light. As I jumped back into shadow I heard yells, shouts and saw figures running wildly around the dock.

Then I heard Polite's voice: "We've got two of them down here with the stuff!"

I ran onto the ship.

Searchlights from the Coast Guard vessel made paths across the water, picking up the smugglers' speedboat, marking its course so the swift *Zev* could follow it. Bullets cracked as the *Zev* unloosed her guns.

Ballinger, meanwhile, came up from the hold of the freighter, dragging with him a thin little Chinese in handcuffs. He was the Number One Boy, who had been lowering the opium through the porthole. Other Agents began to load up the opium tins.

We got into cars that had been waiting nearby and went down to the Customs office.

We learned that the speedboat had been found deserted, and that Sischo, chief of the speedboat crew, was still at large. Agents were put on his trail. Meanwhile, U.S. Deputy Marshals had been sent out to pick up Chin Pak and Chin Wah.

We telephoned Tom Gorman and Ed Shamhart in Washington to report our success. Then we called Gardner in Chicago, asking him to pick up the defendants there and in Detroit.

It was still some hours before dawn when Chin Pak and Chin Wah and I met again—this time at the Federal building. Chin Wah's always mournful face drooped like a bloodhound's.

We stared at each other for a moment and then, with a shrug of resignation, Chin Wah held out his hand. I couldn't shake his hand. It was no longer necessary to pretend friendship.

Chin Pak stood silent and inscrutable. He looked at me coldly but said nothing.

The ring was at last broken—except for Sischo, the speedboat pilot—and he, after weeks of hiding out, gave up and walked in one day to surrender.

We went before the Grand Jury and presented our evidence on which all the defendants were indicted.

They went before Judge John Bowen. All pleaded guilty and received heavy sentences and fines.

In passing sentence, Judge Bowen stated:

"You have pleaded guilty to committing the worst crime on the American statute books.

"It would be impossible for you to have committed a more despicable crime, so far as society is concerned.

"The penalties are not severe enough. I wish I were able to make them more so, but I have given each of you the limit for your offenses under the law. There is only one thing in your favor—you have pleaded guilty and saved the government the expense of a trial."

A Female Racketeer

ALMOST ALL LAW ENFORCE-
ment men have a special aversion for the criminal who is
also a woman.

Part of this feeling is due, no doubt, to idealism. And
some of it comes from bitter experience with women who,
when cornered, often take vicious advantage simply of the
fact of being female.

My own experience taught me that women, if no more
deadly than their male counterparts in crime, are at least
much harder to convict.

Especially when they are beautiful as a woman called
Virginia Cooke.

Virginia was not beautiful in the hard, artificial way
usually associated with the criminal type. She was a natural
blonde, with a slim yet athletic figure. And, when she was
not "on the stuff", she possessed a scrubbed, wholesome
all-American look that made the average male juryman feel
protective.

There were, of course, times when she looked both her
age and her character. But those times never seemed to coin-
cide with her trips to the witness stand.

Virginia was one of the perennial problems of the Customs Service in the port of Seattle. We tangled early and often. In the course of a few years, observing her always from a discreet distance, I learned much about her. I learned about her lovers, too, particularly a swarthy Italian who was also chief liaison man in her personal heroin racket.

But I learned most about her method of operation which, up to that time, was different from the others I had run across.

Virginia made no deliveries, for one thing. In fact, she did not actually sell heroin at all. She sold locker keys—to the small storage lockers that bus depots maintain for the convenience of travelers.

Virginia, or her Italian sweetheart, divided their current supplies of heroin between a certain number of such lockers, deposited the required coins, and carried away the keys. Miles away from the bus depot, they held rendezvous with each eager purchaser in Virginia's expensive car. They negotiated while riding around—and when the price had been settled on and the cash paid, the innocent-looking locker key changed hands. Some time between then and the end of the period covered by the coin deposit, the new possessor of the key claimed his purchase.

Even if we caught the buyer with the drug—and we often did—there was nothing specific to connect him with Virginia. And if he were willing to talk, in the hope of avoiding a stiff Federal sentence, actual proof of what he said would still be lacking.

So we decided to "bring the girl in."

We staked out at her current apartment—(Virginia changed apartments as casually and as often as she did her nail polish) and tried to figure out some way of breaking down her defenses. It wasn't easy. The woman's apartment was her castle and she kept it surrounded by a moat of admirers. Most people who are inaccessible in other ways can be reached by telephone, but Virginia had a way of avoiding that pitfall. She had worked out a telephone signal.

If one of her co-workers wanted to talk to her, he called her number and hung up as soon as the phone buzzed twice. The two rings signalled that a friend was calling. A moment later he called again—then she answered without hesitation.

Later, when I was doing some ticklish undercover work, I had occasion to use this signal myself. It worked without a hitch and I felt rather grateful to Virginia.

The woman never answered the door, either. The door had a bolt with no chain on it, as we found out from the manager of the apartment house—who was a respectable woman—and we decided to try to contact Virginia with the old but still very workable device of delivery service.

Agents Chet Emerick, Polite and I stationed ourselves at the head of the stairs. (Emerick was later Deputy Commissioner of Customs in Washington.)

A Customs Agent in a Western Union uniform got past any lookouts that Virginia may have had and knocked at her door.

"A message for Miss Virginia Cooke."

Waiting at the head of the stairs, we heard her call out: "Shove it under the door."

"Can't. It's a package."

"Oh, the devil with it!"

But curiosity won. She turned the bolt on the door. We rushed in. Her Italian sweetheart sat on the sofa and stared at us open-mouthed. The girl was quicker-witted. She took in the situation in an instant, then reached for her gun. Polite's arm was longer and quicker. Then Virginia burst into fluent profanity.

As I fastened the handcuffs to her lover's lanky wrists, she shouted:

"Listen, if you squawk, I'll treat you worse than the law!"

He must have believed her, for he kept his mouth shut. But we had the narcotics we found in her apartment and her gun for evidence, and we brought her into court.

We really thought she would be convicted—until the day she took the witness stand. We heard the dapper little lawyer who represented her describe her as a "University of Washington coed." Testimony brought out the fact that she had actually attended the University recently for a short time.

Virginia was a born actress. Looking at her, it was hard to believe she was anything but what the attorney represented her to be. Her hair fell smoothly about her face in a long bob. She wore a plain blouse and a plaid wool skirt. Bobby socks and saddle oxfords carried out the schoolgirl theme. Reporters caught her reading Plato during her lunch hour. When her attorney told the jury how these relentless Federal Agents had persecuted her and "planted the stuff" for some unscrupulous reasons of their own, she raised her head and gave me a long, sorrowful look that seemed to express a noble forgiveness.

The sympathetic eyes of the jury followed her glance. I began to fidget. In spite of what I knew beyond all doubt to be the truth, I was beginning to feel a little guilty myself. I looked at Polite. The redness of his neck showed that he felt the same way.

During court recess that day, her Italian friend, who was out on bond awaiting his own trial, came up to me and said proudly:

"What do you think of my gal? She's been off the stuff for a month now."

I knew what the verdict would be before the jury ever came in. Glumly, Polite and I talked over the acquittal at the Customs office. The papers had played up the feminine angle strongly.

"Next time we'll have to catch her in the act—with witnesses," I said.

"If we're lucky," added Girard.

There came a knock at our door. We opened it, and saw

Virginia herself—a high-handed Virginia who obviously was not "off the stuff" anymore and was feeling the full shock of its effects.

"Where," she demanded, "is my root-y-ta-toot?"

Her gun was still in the prosecutor's office. I explained that she could not expect its return. "For one thing, the serial number had been filed off, which makes it illegal."

She made an eloquent gesture. "But, naturally! What earthly good would it be to me with the number on it?"

She flounced out, tapping down the hall in spike-heeled shoes instead of schoolgirl oxfords.

It took us a year but we did it. Not even Virginia could win all the time. Through an informer we heard of a load of heroin that was coming in to San Francisco from the Orient.

On the waterfront we spotted the former "coed". Trailing her car, we followed it from San Francisco to a spot just south of the Washington state line in Oregon. There we "knocked over" her car, with several Oregon police officers present as witnesses to the heroin we seized. We did not want to take a chance on another jury that might have a warm spot for "coeds".

At her second trial, Virginia was convicted and sent to the Federal prison for women in West Virginia. She never returned to the West Coast, to our knowledge. Her Italian companion also took up residence elsewhere, after an interval in a Federal penitentiary.

A Hijacking Swim

In any illegal racket, there are always the hijackers—the sly operators who make a precarious living cutting themselves in, violently or otherwise, on the smuggler's haul.

They usually meet death early, but while they live and practice their racket, they provide endless complications for a Customs Agent's work.

I recall only one instance in which a professional hijacker played on our team—and brought us three hundred cans of opium at a cost, to the American taxpayer, of one dollar a can.

It was December 1, 1935. We were in Seattle when I got a wire from our Shanghai agent, telling me that the SS *Tantalus* of the Blue Funnel Line was due in port by the middle of the month and that three hundred cans of opium were known to be concealed somewhere aboard.

We went out by Coast Guard cutter and met the *Tantalus* just off Port Townsend. We followed her in to make certain no contraband could be dropped without discovery. When she reached port we put a double guard on the dock, and ordered that anyone and anything coming ashore be minutely examined. Then we went aboard with a trained searching party of eleven men. Even the resident cockroaches were annoyed by the examination we gave their ship.

But we found nothing.

"Well?" I asked Agent Polite.

He grinned. "Corky says it's aboard, so it's got to be there."

He was right. Corky never erred. If he had been trying to tip us on horse races instead of contraband we might all have retired rich. We launched three canoes and maintained a twenty-four-hour vigil beneath the pier. Anyone attempting to enter the slips on either side would be clearly silhouetted.

When the *Tantalus* shifted to a lumber company's dock at Everett, she docked with port side next to the pier.

An all-night watch in a canoe is anything but a lark. You can't move much for fear of throwing the canoe off balance. There is no protection against the weather. Polite and I took up our watch daily at sunset, wearing long woolen underwear against the winter cold, with two pairs of socks each, our heaviest sweaters, mackinaws and gloves. Still, we froze. Long before dawn each morning we had emptied our gallon thermos of coffee. The rest of the watch was sheer misery.

It was 2:30 a.m. on the second night at Everett that we saw the dim outline of a canoe beyond the sea side of the ship. It headed toward us, then turned, skirted the side of the *Tantalus* and disappeared again beyond the stern without stopping. Either it was a trial run or else its occupants intended to pick up the narcotics on the other, or starboard, side of the ship.

Polite and I dug in our paddles. As we drew near the ship's stern we heard a series of soft splashes and knew the canoe was returning. We pulled up beside them, and said quietly, "Customs Agents. Put them up."

Surprise prevented any escape attempt. Their hands

were up obediently, but one of the men, seated in the stern, growled, "Can't a fellow go night-fishing without a couple of you nosy characters butting in?"

The voice—low, husky, with a note of hill country humor even under those circumstances—was familiar. I turned my flashlight on him. The face was familiar, too—Len Wyddell, former hop peddler for the Wong syndicate. He recently had been paroled from an armed burglary rap.

"Depends on what you're fishing for," I told him. "It's closed season on opium, Len."

His answering chuckle showed that he recognized my voice, too. But he kept silent. We had tangled before. He was ruthless, clever, highly ingenious. But he also had a streak of real courage—rare in the smuggling circles—and it didn't take a shot in the arm to put it into action.

We brought both men to shore. Len's companion proved to be a parolee also, and the gun he carried was enough to send him back to finish his term.

As parolee Wyddell also had a gun, we left him to stew incommunicado all night. In the morning we brought him into our office, hoping to get him to talk. We asked him what he thought we should do with him.

Surprisingly, he asked bluntly:

"Interested in a trade?"

"What kind?"

"The dope you're after for five century notes," he replied.

We considered. "That's a lot, Wyddell."

"Four, then."

"Make it three and you've got yourself a deal," we told him.

He hesitated, licked his lips, and began to talk.

"I got this info—don't ask me where—of how the Number One Boy on the *Tantalus* had charge of the shipment this time and how he was going to get it off.

"Every night since they docked at Seattle he's been letting a black fishline out of number six starboard porthole. He's going to keep on doing it at Everett until a sock with three triangular holes cut in it is stuck on the hook and someone jerks the line. He'll reel it in, check the signal, then attach the cans, all tied together in the usual long sausage, and lower it out the porthole.

"They figured the pick-up men would be in a canoe, but I had an idea you were on to the shipment and there wasn't a chance in hades to get it. So, for the past three weeks I've been swallowing cod liver oil like it was booze."

"Cod liver oil?" Ballinger's voice was incredulous. "Why that?"

He explained slowly. "To raise the temperature of my blood. My racket called for taking a swim, and you know Puget Sound in winter would freeze boiling water. So I was going to swim from under the dock around the ship and pick up the dope. And I'll do it this very night if you'll just give me the dough first."

There was a mirror in the room. Glancing at it I saw my mouth hanging open. Recovering my voice, I remarked:

"The Wongs should have paid you well for that."

"No," he answered, "I intended taking it all for myself this time."

"Hijacking it, eh?" said Polite.

"Sure, if you guys hadn't queered it."

We sent Len into an anteroom under guard. After talking it over we agreed we had nothing to lose by trying it out.

We called Wyddell back in. "It's a deal," we told him.

We gave him the money—three hundred dollars in mint-fresh bills. The man folded them with obvious satisfaction. Remembering the cold of the Sound, I wondered if he would live to spend it.

"You'd better have one more swig of that oil," I told him.

He grinned. "Don't worry about me, Hanks. I drank so much on the way over I can feel fish scales growing where my skin ought to be."

That night Ballinger, Polite, Wyddell and I went down to our waterfront office. Len stripped, smeared on a thick layer of grease and wrapped himself in a blanket. He and I got in one canoe, Ballinger and Polite in another.

We paddled quietly under the pier to a point opposite the number six porthole on the port side. Wyddell handed me one end of a long line he had brought along. He looped the other end of it around his shoulders. Then, naked, he eased himself out of the canoe into the frigid water and swam quietly around the ship's bow.

Up to then I had been confident that I could see a swimmer thirty feet away on even the darkest night. I found I was wrong. Before Wyddell had taken a dozen strokes he was invisible. I could only wait and play out the line, allowing plenty of slack so as not to interfere with the swimmer.

Polite and Ballinger in their canoe—I in mine—waited while Wyddell slid through the icy water around the bow to the starboard side of the *Tantalus*, found the fishline and attached to it the signal sock he carried. We waited—while the Number One Boy cautiously pulled in his line, identified the token, and let down the contraband. As it sank it was heavy enough to pull the line under the ship's keel so it would not become fouled.

For Wyddell those moments must have been sheer agony. Some time later he came alongside and I helped him into the canoe. His teeth chattered so he could hardly clamp them firmly enough to pull out the cork of his whisky bottle.

I began pulling on the line he had given me. Hand over hand I drew it in. Then the harvest began—sausage after sausage of opium cans, enough to fill both our canoes.

Even when the three hundred cans were safely aboard, our night's work was not over. Hastily we paddled ashore, turned Wyddell and the contraband over to a guard, then ran down the pier and up the ship's gangplank.

Down in the crew's quarters every member of the Chinese crew lay apparently asleep, some snoring loudly. We went from one bunk to another with our flashlights and eventually found one who was not only fully dressed under his blankets, but dripping with perspiration. It was the Number One Boy. When pressed, he showed us an open manhole leading to a cleverly-made hiding place in one of the hollow beams.

It was a great night for the Customs Service—a worthwhile night for Len Wyddell, too. Perhaps the dangers of his freezing swim gave him a needed faith in himself. Perhaps it was the three hundred dollars that gave him his start. For whatever reason, Len is a law-abiding man today—one of the very few of the many lawbreakers I have known who-ever reformed and made the conversion stick.

The Rum Runners

Since my career was concerned almost entirely with narcotic smuggling, I handled fewer liquor smuggling cases than did the average Agent. But I saw enough of it to learn that while the Customs Service was adept in distinguishing between the amateur and the professional in rum-running, the general public made no such distinction. The smugglers of liquor were difficult to catch in the first place—there were so many of them and so few of us. And to get convictions, particularly when the defendants were tried by jury, was even more difficult.

The local administration of the Volstead Act was none of our concern. Our job was to stave off the ships slipping in from Mexico, Canada, or even from Europe, whose sole business was to haul liquor to supply the flourishing illicit trade.

During the Prohibition era, the *Pescawha* was one of the busiest ships in the smuggling racket. Her Canadian skipper, Bob Phamplett, had unloaded enough liquor on the West Coast to set him up for a lifetime in McNeil—if he could be caught in the act. So far, we had not. He never hit the same beach twice in succession, and we could not cover all the coves and inlets a small boat might enter.

While awaiting contact with his friends on shore, it was

Phamplett's practice to cruise just outside the mouth of the Columbia river, only yards beyond the legal limit of seizure. In February one year, he was cruising thus and we were watching him as usual with binoculars when a squall blew up.

In the rough water, a fisherman's gasboat capsized not far from where the *Pescawha* was riding the swell. The Canadian vessel moved into the mouth of the river, inside the legal limit, and began picking up the crew.

At the same time, the Coast Guard cutter *Algonquin,* proceeding seaward from Astoria, Oregon, to rescue the fishermen, and seeing the *Pescawha* inside the lawful limit, overtook and boarded her. The cargo of a thousand cases of whisky was confiscated, and her captain and crew put under arrest and turned over to Customs.

Then the storm broke over our heads.

Portland proclaimed Phamplett a hero. A Canadian, he had disregarded possible arrest and imprisonment in an attempt to rescue American fishermen. By public subscription, a watch was bought for him. It was inscribed "To A Hero" and was presented to him ceremoniously. Newspapers published photos across the country; interviews were given; public opinion blasted the government's action, making it appear that the Treasury men had taken advantage of an heroic act for their own arbitrary purposes.

Public opinion was such that we felt there was no chance of conviction if the Government were to proceed to immediate trial. George Neuner, the fighting U.S. attorney of Portland, wanted a thorough investigation that might enable him to get convictions of all involved.

An excellent Treasury investigator, H. M. Dengler, was assigned in charge of the case. Together, we spent almost a year on it before we broke it. Finally, we learned a few facts about Phamplett's method of disposing of the liquor.

It involved a speedboat, the *Azalea,* and a ferryboat

which crossed the Columbia River on scheduled trips between Kalama, Washington, and Rainier, Oregon. These towns were approximately fifty miles up the river from Astoria. This ferry stopped running at eight o'clock at night. Some time after that, by arrangement with the owners, one of the rum runner's men ran the ferry out into mid-river. Here it kept rendezvous with the *Azalea*, which had proceeded upstream with liquor from the *Pescawha*.

While the cases of liquor were unloaded, trucks gathered on either side of the river. The method was ingenious. If Federal agents appeared on one side, the load could be switched to the other.

When we had information that a load was coming in on a particular night, we contacted prohibition agents and all other enforcement officers we could get, manned each side of the river and went into action. We got the liquor, the trucks, the ferryboat and the *Azalea*. More important, we obtained a great amount of evidence involving Phamplett.

Federal attorney Neuner conducted the trial so skillfully that all persons involved were convicted and sentenced.

❋   ❋   ❋   ❋   ❋   ❋   ❋   ❋   ❋   ❋   ❋   ❋

My favorite story of prohibition times concerns me hardly at all, and the smuggling of liquor was involved only indirectly.

At the time I was stationed in Seattle. One day a woman telephoned my office to complain that someone was using a ranch near hers as a storehouse for smuggled liquor.

This was not the first time I had spoken to this woman. Three months before, through her tipoff, we had captured a large consignment of liquor on this same ranch. So I thanked her, told her she would be rewarded if we effected a capture, and assurred her we would look into the matter immediately.

Nevertheless, I was doubtful. The ranch was known to be "hot", and would not likely be used again so soon.

So, contrary to practice, I sent only one man, instead of the usual pair.

To reach this ranch, one had to leave town to the north, make several turns and turn again at an old cemetery. There were plenty of hiding places along this tree-lined dirt road. The agent, a young recruit by the name of Bellinger, parked his car in a thicket and crept to a spot where he could watch the entrance to the ranch.

He had been there only long enough for the motor of his car to cool off when he saw a Ford coupe with only the driver in it, come out of the yard, pass his hiding place and head south for Seattle.

Bellinger hurried to his car and trailed the Ford for several miles. Then he saw it stop where a road ran through a thick forest.

One of the first rules taught us in law enforcement is that, when trailing a car, the agent must take the initiative. He must overtake and order the other car to stop. But Bellinger was new at the game and excited over his first solo assignment. He stopped his car back of the Ford, got out, ran forward and drew his gun.

"Get out and unlock the back end of the car," he ordered.

The man obeyed docilely enough. To Bellinger's astonishment the trunk was filled with machine guns. It looked like a miniature arsenal.

Bellinger made the mistake of leaning forward for a closer look. . . .

When he came to his senses he was locked in the trunk of the car.

His wrists were manacled together by his own handcuffs. The machine guns had disappeared. As the car ate up the miles, he could hear—dimly—two occupants in the front seat talking.

One—whose name Bellinger later learned was Manning

—was trying to convince the other—named Olsen—that they ought to kill their passenger.

"He's seen me in the car. He's bound to identify me when he gets the chance."

But Olsen "didn't hold with killing anyone. Not even the law—except as a last resort." They would escape, he said soothingly, without committing "another murder."

Before Bellinger had digested the word "another", Olsen advanced a different argument—one which made the officer's ear drums ring.

"Who was it robbed the bank, huh? Who got away with the cabbage, huh? And who cut you in, huh? This is my show and I'm running it my way."

A week before, a bank had been robbed in Vancouver, B. C. Both teller and cashier had been killed and over $35,000 stolen. It was now clear to Bellinger that it was this money that had been cached at the ranch, and not liquor. What was not clear was why Olsen should have no scruples about killing tellers and cashiers, but drew the line at law enforcement officers. Clear or not, he was heartily in favor of Olsen's discrimination!

The ride went on and on. The lick that Manning had given Bellinger made his head ache and he had a violent thirst. At times he was conscious and then a quick jolt would bang his head against the top of the trunk and he would be out again. Every bump and rut bounced him from one side of the trunk to the other. He had no way of computing the passing of time.

Once he knew they were passing through a large town because he heard streetcar gongs. Also the car stopped abruptly several times for what must have been traffic lights, and there was a welcome absence of rough bumps.

He deduced that this must be Portland, since the only other place near Seattle large enough to have streetcars was

Vancouver, B. C., and Bellinger was sure they had not crossed the border. That would have meant inspection, the trunk would have been opened, and he would have been discovered.

So they were driving south.

He had been stuffed into his prison about eight o'clock in the morning. It was evening and over five hundred miles farther south when the car stopped and the trunk cover was flung up.

Bellinger blinked at the sunshine which momentarily blinded him. The two men, their faces concealed by handkerchief masks, pulled him out. Each taking an arm, they half-pulled, half-carried him to a small tree about half a mile from the highway.

Then one of the pair—Bellinger decided it was Manning—fished out the key to the handcuffs. He loosened one of the Agent's arms, only to refasten the cuffs again so that Bellinger was now hugging the tree. Grinning maliciously, the villain put the key tantalizingly near, in sight, yet completely out of reach. Then the two men returned to the car and drove away, still apparently heading south.

No one had said anything during this episode. Tortured by thirst, still dazed from the jolting he had received, Bellinger looked dizzily around. He was in a forest, a long way off the highway, with no house in sight. It was a question whether he could make his shouts heard. If he could not, there was a strong chance he might starve to death.

He waited until he heard a car approaching, then desperately moistening his parched lips, began to shout.

The car was too far away. It rolled by without stopping.

Back in Seattle that same night, I got a phone call. A car, stopping to change a tire, had heard Bellinger's shouts and released him. He was in Ashland, Oregon. Shakily, he told me all that had happened, gave me the license number of the car, and also a sketchy description of Olsen and Manning.

"Are you all right?" I asked him. He was quite young, and I couldn't forget I had sent him out alone on a mission that might have meant his death.

He answered jauntily, "Sure, I'm o.k. I'm taking the next bus home. Just you catch those fellows—"

We issued an all-points bulletin for all officers to be on the lookout for the car. We also ordered the license number traced. Then I waited all night at my desk. But no news came.

At eight o'clock I went out for an unsatisfactory breakfast. It was Sunday and I should have been at home. When I returned there was a report on the license. It was registered to a very reputable Ford dealer in Seattle.

The dealer got out of bed and hustled down to his office. After checking his sales records he discovered that a week before, two strangers had come in to buy a car. They were ready to pay all cash. He had been unable to make immediate delivery on the model they wanted, but at their insistence he had accepted their money and loaned them a coupe—the one with the license number in question. Although the new car had then been ready for delivery for several days, the customers had not returned.

The dealer's books proved his statements. The customers' names were listed as Jones and Smith, obviously false.

Moments later, a telegram was handed me. Sent from Los Angeles, it was unsigned, and told the approximate spot where Bellinger had been left handcuffed. Quickly I telephoned the main Los Angeles office of Western Union. But the telegram had been turned in to the office by a messenger and they could tell us nothing.

Who had sent it—Jones or Smith, Olsen or Manning? From Bellinger's description of their conversation and actions, I decided it was Olsen.

Another all-points bulletin went out, this time including Los Angeles and San Diego, as well as the Mexican border.

We received a surprisingly quick report. This time it was from an officer of the California State Plant Inspection Service, phoning from Hilt, the inspection station at the California-Oregon border.

"Your car's just been through inspection, going south. Its occupants were a man about thirty and a boy not over nineteen. Very poorly dressed. I couldn't hold it—had no authority—as it held no contraband, no weapons, or even sacks of seeds."

But, he said, he had dragged out the inspection as long as possible and managed, during it, to duck into his office and call the sheriff at Yreka. Since the car headed south, the sheriff should meet it at any moment. He was positive the man and boy were unarmed.

The report of the car's occupants puzzled me. The older man might well be Manning. It matched well enough with the description given by the Ford dealer. But who was the boy? And what had happened to Olsen?

Soon after that, the little town of Yreka spent the bloodiest and most exciting Sabbath morning of its slightly somnolent history.

After talking to the inspector, the sheriff had telephoned a California state highway patrolman at a small garage outside Hornbrook.

"Stop Manning when he comes through—or follow and overtake him if he gets past you."

As the highway officer left the phone, the attendant at the gas pump reported that a Ford coupe had just flashed by "doing better than sixty."

The patrolman ran for his car. The attendant begged permission to go along. The officer nodded and they started south with siren shrieking. They raced ahead at sixty-five —seventy.

Ten miles later they caught up with the coupe. The officer had held the gas pedal to the floor until they drew abreast of it. Now he shouted to the driver to "pull over". But the "unarmed" driver answered with a volley of shot, and the patrolman slumped dead in the seat.

The gas station attendant grabbed for the wheel. Another shot got him also. The police car, out of control, careened off the road and turned over.

Manning sped on without stopping—and met the sheriff's car racing north. The sheriff took in the scene at once. He exchanged shots with Manning—all shots going wild—and swung his car around in pursuit. He radioed his office and ordered a posse formed and the road blocked at Yreka, ten miles ahead.

The deputy who took the message dashed out into the street to enlist every man in sight. They swung a truck sidewise to block the highway. They got out rifles, revolvers and shotguns, and took shelter behind trees and in shop doorways.

Seconds later, Manning's coupe roared into view. He stopped inches short of the truck, swung his car boldly onto the sidewalk, skirted the roadblock and was on his way again. But before he could pick up speed the posse began to fire. The volley broke the car windows, sieved the chassis, and punctured a tire. Steering with one hand, Manning fired with the other, until a shot caught him in the chest. The car slid to a stop.

As it slowed down, the door opened. The boy dashed out, ran through a hail of bullets into a drug store and ducked under a counter. To the angry armed men who followed him in he pleaded, "I surrender, I surrender—just don't shoot me, please."

And then he fainted. They carted him off to jail. Meanwhile, Manning, who miraculously was not dead, was taken to a hospital.

Some of the threads of this story can be as securely tied as the final chapters of a mystery novel. Others will never be unraveled.

We surmised that, after chaining Bellinger to the tree, the pair of kidnappers had gone to some airport from which Olsen had caught a plane for Los Angeles.

We know that Manning spent the night at a motel in Medford, Oregon, because that was where he picked up the boy.

The youth told us his story. He had been hitch-hiking when Manning offered him a lift. Just before arriving at the plant inspection station the man had given him three automatics and said: "Hide these in your pockets 'til we're over the line."

The boy did not know why the inspector had not spotted the guns in his bulging pockets.

"Maybe he thought I wasn't the type to carry a pistol."

He was not the type, it was true—and he had had enough dangerous excitement for his whole life.

Another knot was tied when Bellinger went back to the ranch with another agent to retrieve his car. The machine guns had been cached nearby where he had been kidnapped.

Manning was indicted for murder. When the trial started, several of the most highly-paid criminal lawyers in the country arrived to defend him. After he was found guilty, his case was appealed from court to court, and after three years reached the U.S. Supreme Court. There he lost. Manning eventually was executed.

Where had the money for his defense come from? Ostensibly from Manning's feminine friend in Seattle. Investigation showed, however, that she had little money. We guessed at Olsen.

Immediately after Manning's arrest, we had found out where his sweetheart lived and had maintained close surveillance over her actions, associates and correspondence. When a letter arrived postmarked Los Angeles, we suspected that Olsen was the sender. So we telephoned the address that the letter-writer had carelessly put on the envelope to our Los Angeles office. Two agents there were detailed to follow it up.

They found Olsen. At that time the Federal government and the Los Angeles authorities were feuding, the government claiming that the amount charged by the county jail for keeping Federal prisoners was exorbitant. Olsen, though a suspected murderer and bank robber, was placed in the small suburban jail at Glendale.

This was late one evening. Next morning, after the two agents had secured the proper papers, they returned to the jail to take their prisoner before the U.S. Commissioner. But Olsen was nowhere to be found!

What had happened was that he had been put in the cell for drunks because the jail was so crowded. He soon learned that drunken inmates were set free as soon as they sobered up if they could produce bail. So Olsen changed clothes with an unconscious inebriate. When the jailer appeared, Olsen produced his bail and was freed. He walked out the door just a few minutes before the two agents arrived.

In the following months several banks in the Los Angeles area were robbed. Simultaneously, the money for Manning's defense appeared.

Later, Olsen was apprehended again. He eventually received a total of ninety years in the penitentiary on the bank holdup charges.

A Creature From The Deep

WE WERE WORKING ON A Japanese case that spring, "staking out" an isolated cove where we had reason to think that a certain boat might put in with a load of heroin.

I stood the eight to two a.m. shift. My way home took me past a boat-house owned by a Chinese called "Turkey".

For a long time we had suspected Turkey of narcotics skullduggery and, since the hour was favorable when I passed his place, I began to make a practice of giving it the once-over.

Sometimes I drove past slowly, watching for boats that might be tied up at his dock. Other times, when the weather was pleasant and my bottle of coffee had lasted long enough to keep me awake, I'd park my car in the grove of trees down the highway and survey the place on foot.

The beat I worked out for myself took me behind the boat-house to a vantage point where I could see not only the piling of his rickety dock but the water beneath it as well. By lying flat on the ground, where I could not be seen from the house, and waiting until my eyes became accustomed to the darkness, I could study anything in the vicinity.

I was lying thus one night when something happened which jolted me upright.

113

From the star-lit water that lapped the slimy piling, two great arms were suddenly uplifted. A huge round head followed. For almost two minutes arms and head remained out-thrust above the water, in grotesque movements I could not comprehend.

Then the head quickly sank from sight. The arms followed. There was nothing left but water, rising and falling quietly as if nothing had disturbed its tranquillity.

This was in 1934, before the days of space travel. But having read Jules Verne, H. G. Wells and others, I began to think that all these ideas of people from another planet might have some reality.

I waited at least half an hour, but nothing else happened. Finally I decided to walk down to the dock.

No one was there. I leaned over the edge of the pier and stared into the water. The apparition had vanished.

The next day I told Polite about it. His reaction was exactly as tolerant as I expected it to be. "I'll meet you there at two tomorrow morning, Mel. I want to get a look at this thing!"

That was the first of many watches we kept at the boat-house—but with no more weird figures emerging from the water, the weather growing more and more unpleasant, and Polite—I felt—less and less sure I had seen anything at all. Not that he ever said as much. He just ceased to look expectant. I had the feeling he was humoring me by being there at all.

Then one night the hand again rose out of the water so close to where we had put our thermos that we thought our man from Mars was reaching for a drink. The enormous head followed. The hand then looped a rope expertly round a spike and disappeared.

I looked at Girard triumphantly. But we neither spoke nor moved.

Moments later a square black box rose on the rope, followed by the whole of the incredible body of the stranger from out of the sea.

We had our hands on our pistols, ready for anything. Suddenly the grotesque head turned toward us—and then a smothered explosion of Chinese profanity shook the air. We recognized the voice of Turkey.

What followed was anti-climax. We moved toward him, guns leveled, and he lifted the gigantic hands in surrender. I tried to lift off the preposterous helmet, but it was fastened on the inside. At last I had to let the Chinese do it himself.

"This box," said Polite, "contains a fancy load of hero-in!"

So we confiscated it, locked it in the trunk of the car, and then took Turkey to his boat-house. While he got into clothing more suitable for going to jail, we examined his diving suit with growing interest.

We had never seen anything like it before. No oxygen hose, which would have required someone on shore to keep him supplied with air, but instead, it had a built-in oxygen tank—making the size of the suit enormous—which would supply air under water for forty minutes.

"Where'd you get this contraption, Turkey?"

Swearing and sniffling alternately, he told us. It all came about when he had attended the World's Fair in Chicago with some of his compatriots. While they were entertaining themselves with various kinds of frivolity, Turkey had explored the exhibits of scientific invention.

There the diving suit had caught his eye. When the Fair was over he had negotiated with the inventor, who had not found a sponsor and was willing to let the suit go for a few thousand dollars. Turkey paid gladly. He had a plan for the thing. It was an ingenious one, too.

When a dope-carrying ship came into port, Turkey

would put on his diving suit and walk under the water from his boathouse near the pier where the vessel was docked. There he would find the inevitable fishline let down by the Number One Chinese Boy. After Turkey signalled properly by jerking on the line, a waterproofed package would be lowered to the bottom of the harbor where he was waiting.

Aware that any place near the waterfront was liable to suspicion when a foreign vessel was in, Turkey always used great caution. Carefully, the Chinese would tie his prize to the submerged piling. There, hidden under water, it would bob with the current for a week, two weeks, even a month—until Turkey figured the heat was off and it was safe to bring the package to the surface at his own private dock.

That was what he had been doing the first time I saw him rising from the water.

The heroin was worth, at that time, about $30,000. We took it and Turkey into town. Eventually he joined some of his other friends at McNeil Island.

As for the suit, we confiscated it. Now it is once more part of an exhibit—this time under the auspices of the United States government, and not "For Sale".

Border Gold

HISTORY DOES NOT VERIFY this thesis, but I have always felt that Diogenes must have been in the Greek Customs Service.

His lantern is the tip-off. He probably used it—not so much to search for an honest man—as to poke around the cargoes in the holds of galleys and feluccas, or to probe incoming chariots at the borders of Athens.

An Agent's electric torch is, of course, a modern improvement over the lantern—but, to even things up, it has to penetrate deeper. In Diogenes' day there were fewer things to smuggle. There were no laws then against collecting the juice of poppies, and the gods themselves were in the liquor business and no believers in prohibition.

Yet even then, gold was doubtless subject to a heavy importation tax, and for that reason was very likely taken in secret from one city to another.

And gold is still being smuggled. This report would not be complete without describing some of the ingenious gold smugglers I have met.

In July, 1938, an ex-rum smuggler who had always played both ends against the middle by doubling as an informer, came to my office in Seattle.

As usual, he had information for me and expected to be well paid for divulging it. Also, as usual, it took half an hour's haggling to reach an agreement. Whereupon he told me this story:

The previous night he had entertained an unexpected visitor, an "old gink who looked like one of them profs out at the University."

This "old gink" carried a letter of introduction from a former liquor supply connection in Vancouver, B. C. Speaking with an accent, he told my informer that he had approximately one hundred and fifty thousand dollars in gold bars cached across the Canadian border.

He could, of course, sell it openly there, but he wanted the higher price obtainable in the United States. He was prepared to smuggle it in if Vic—my informant—would guarantee to buy it on its arrival.

Vic agreed to try to put it over. He probably visited every gold broker in town before he decided the only profit he could make was by playing ball with Customs. He stalled the visitor—whom he called Smith—and Smith agreed to wait twenty-four hours for an answer.

"So what," asked Vic," do you want me to do, and what are you going to pay me to do it?"

Assistant Collector of Customs Ballinger and I went into conference. We told Vic to go ahead with his deal to buy the gold if it was brought across the border, and also to inform us when the attempt to smuggle it in would be made.

Next morning he came into our office grinning. He had seen Smith. The older man was driving back to Vancouver by auto and would return the next evening with the gold. Vic had both the license number and make of the car, as well as a good description of the occupant.

Agents Bradt and Atherton went to Blaine, the inspection point on the American side of the border. They began searching all cars when they saw Smith's vehicle coming into sight. In this way Smith would not think his car was being singled out, and so would not put the finger on Vic.

Bradt and Atherton carried out their part well. Smith cheerfully allowed them to search, looking at them with an expression of intelligent interest on his face. He was indeed a scholarly-looking gentleman, dignified, with an air of impeccable respectability. Under ordinary circumstances his car would have been passed with but a cursory examination.

Even now they began to think a mistake had been made. There were no gold bars in any of the usual hiding places. But the springs sagged in the rear—and above them they found a built-in compartment with twenty gold bars over each wheel.

They brought Smith in to jail in Seattle and locked the gold up in our office safe. We were skeptical that the bars were genuine. It seemed highly unlikely that the scholarly old man could have accumulated that much valuable metal, lawfully or otherwise. But the assay showed the bars to be true gold.

Now the unusual facets of the story became known:

First, Smith confessed that although the bars in the car were worth fifty thousand dollars, he had another hundred thousand worth still cached in Canada. He told us of its hiding place, and Atherton at once drove up to Vancouver. He told the Royal Canadian Mounted Police of its location and watched while they confiscated the treasure.

Where Smith had secured the gold was a story in itself.

Our dignified gentleman had been a supervisor in a large gold mine in New Zealand for twenty years. Each day he had stolen a small amount of gold—so small that he could easily cover its disappearance on the records. He had saved these daily thefts systematically, pending his retirement, when he dreamed of going to America, to live in luxury for the rest of his life.

There were three extraordinary things about this confession. One, that he had been able to steal this gold over such a long period without detection; two, that he had saved the metal instead of succumbing to the temptation to squander it; three, that he had managed to smuggle this gold from New Zealand to Australia—which has an excellent Customs system—from Australia into Canada and from Canada, almost, into the United States.

No doubt he would have crossed our border successfully had he not arranged to sell his treasure to an informer.

The government brought Smith to trial. He pleaded guilty and was sentenced to McNeil Island Federal penitentiary for eighteen months. After serving this term he was turned over to the New Zealand authorities who, in the interim, had obtained extradition papers.

All of the gold was claimed by New Zealand. Canada also claimed it. Up to now, the case has never been decided. Meanwhile, Canada is holding the $100,000 she confiscated, and the United States has the $50,000 seized at the border.

The only person who got any actual cash out of the "old gink's" twenty years of gold-pinching was Vic, our informer. The government paid him off the day after Smith's arrest.

❋   ❋   ❋   ❋   ❋   ❋   ❋   ❋

Another tip on a gold-smuggling venture came to us from the Canadian Royal Mounted.

This organization deserves credit in any account dealing with the war against smugglers. It is an honest, efficient and vigilant group of men. The Canadian Royal Mounted Police have given us many a tip-off, with no informer's fee expected. Of course they are powerless to make arrests south of the Line, and we cannot pursue our suspects even six inches north of the border—but we can lawfully exchange information with each other, which we did regularly.

It was in 1936 that John Healey, one of my Royal friends, telephoned me that two Yugoslavs in Vancouver had somehow come into possession of a large amount of gold bullion which they were preparing to smuggle into the United States.

"They have a room on the seventh floor of the Georgia Hotel," he told me. "Come up to Vancouver and we'll see what we can find out about their plans."

A "Mountie" asks for something and he gets it. Within fifteen minutes after my arrival John had rented a room on the same floor as our suspects. He arranged with the desk clerk to be notified whenever they left the hotel. Plans were made that when this happened, all elevators would be held for ten minutes on whatever pretext might be deemed necessary. Healey also arranged for a pass key.

We sat in our room, reminiscing and waiting. But when the clerk phoned that our men had gone out, we went into action. Opening their door, we quickly installed a dictograph in the room and connected it with a listening device in ours. Half an hour later, with the ten minutes of extra time provided by the stalled elevators, the two Serbs reentered their room. At once they began to discuss how they were going to get "it" into Seattle.

After talking over various methods, they finally decided that the best way was to take the bus. First, they would distribute "it" evenly by sewing "it" into layers in their long underwear. They would make the layers a quarter of an inch thick so that there would be no betraying bulges. They also decided that, to disarm the inspectors, they would carry nothing in their hands and bring no baggage.

Unfortunately they did not mention which bus they would take. Patience was forced upon us. Healey went back to his barracks and I went down to the lobby, picked out the most restful chair and waited. On through the afternoon and until dinner time I waited. Then my stomach began clamoring for attention. Since I did not dare leave the lobby even long enough to visit the coffee shop, I had to be satisfied with three chocolate bars, a package of peanuts, and an evening paper, all of which could be purchased at the newsstand.

All night I waited, changing chairs occasionally, dozing off when the lobby was empty but waking instantly each time the elevator stopped. At dawn the scrubwomen scrubbed the floors and emptied the cuspidors; the day shift came on; the restaurant opened and the air was filled with the tantalizing fragrance of fresh, hot coffee. I yearned to bribe a bellhop to bring me a cup but did not want to arouse his curiosity.

Then my patience reaped its reward. The suspects came out of the elevator and walked briskly through the lobby. Their destination, to my delight, was the coffee shop. I followed, and the three of us had breakfast.

After they had finished, paid their checks, and selected toothpicks, they went to the bus station. I followed them onto the bus and sat behind them.

For the two would-be smugglers, filled with hope and excitement, it was an enjoyable ride—until they reached the border. There I asked the Customs Inspectors to take them into the Customs house and search them.

Strips of "it" were indeed sewn to their long underwear. They made the remainder of the trip to Seattle in a Bureau car, handcuffed.

I went with them, but in the city we separated. They were taken to the county jail, minus their union suits which were left in the office safe, and I went home to sleep soundly until morning.

Next day we listened to their story—one compounded equally of humor, pathos, and the ever-present ingredient of avarice.

The Yugoslavs were day laborers who had worked in

and around Vancouver for the previous ten years. During that time they had carefully saved their money in the hope that eventually they might return to their native land and live on their savings. They figured it would take them at least another decade before they would be able to realize their plans. Then they met a fellow countryman who seemed wealthy and offered to let them, as compatriots, participate in a "good thing."

He took them to an open field where he was sure he would not be overheard, and spoke in whispers to make assurance doubly positive.

He had, he told them, discovered a gold mine "somewhere in British Columbia"—a mine so stuffed with gold that he almost blushed each time he drove in his pick. His only problem was how to dispose of this abundance. If he offered it to the authorities they would demand taxes. But he was a Yugoslav, not a Canadian, and he did not care to pay taxes to a foreign government. Rather than do so he would sell his gold to his new friends for the bargain price of ten dollars an ounce.

"How much did you say?" I asked, unbelieving.

"Ten dollars an ounce."

Apparently they saw nothing ridiculous about this. The current quotation on gold was $32.00 an ounce.

We sent the pair back to jail and took a sample of the gold to a chemist. They had rightly referred to their purchase as "it". The stuff they had smuggled into the United States was small bits of plain, ordinary lead which had been given a thin coating of gold.

In spite of myself I felt sorry for them. Obviously, they were not professional crooks—just two poor, hardworking, but gullible chaps who had been bilked by someone who spoke their language and who took advantage of their greed. But they had broken our smuggling laws, and every such violation must go before the Grand Jury. So they had to stay in jail until there was another session of that body, at which time we presented the facts.

The jurors were interested in the case and duly considered all the circumstances. On the recommendation of the U.S. attorney, they returned a "no true bill".

The two Yugoslavs left hastily for Canada, fully determined to find their "friend" and liquidate him. I notified John Healey of their departure and told him of the threats they had made.

But John, when I next saw him, had no murder to report. Perhaps the bilker had already sailed to his homeland, with new ideas on selling his countrymen more lead washed with gold.

Spies and Smugglers

THE BATTLE BETWEEN LAW and law-breaker is constant. New methods and techniques may be developed and used by the combatants, but the conflict itself remains unchanged.

In the mid-thirties, we on the Pacific coast began to feel a change in the international status of things.

The tide of narcotics flowed as strong as ever from the Orient to our shores, but its source had shifted. Even the faces of the smugglers had changed. Round countenances gave way to bony ones. Slanted eyes were more likely to be shielded by spectacles. The Japanese, who up until then had given us only minor trouble, began moving into the narcotics racket in a big way. The Customs Bureau was now shuttling me up and down the West Coast.

Looking back now, the reasons are clear. The Japanese, with their usual feeling for economy, had combined narcotics smuggling and espionage in one ingenious operation. The first enterprise supplied financial support for the second. The same personnel served in two capacities.

One of the incidents pointing up the change in the narcotics situation was the case of the Ogata baby's diapers.

Papa Ogata was one of the many thousands of Japanese

citizens who, before World War II, lived on the Pacific coast. Prevented from becoming naturalized citizens by the U.S. Oriental exclusion laws, a few of these Nipponese remained technical and sometimes enthusiastic subjects of their Emperor.

Their children, born American citizens, and educated in American schools, proved preponderantly loyal to the country of their birth. Only a minority of the older people were ever suspected of outright sedition. This minority, however, was able to cause considerable trouble before the Pearl Harbor catastrophe resulted in confinement of all Japanese in concentration camps for the war's duration.

In the late thirties, some of these Japanese-Americans found a ready and lucrative berth in the Nipponese illicit trade in narcotics.

Ogata was one of these. But, like most Japanese, he lacked the finesse that made Chinese smugglers such interesting problems. So eventually, we caught up with him, confiscated his stockpile of morphine, and deported him to Japan.

Mama Ogata and six-months-old Oriji dutifully accompanied him back to the land of the Rising Sun.

But a few months later, claiming their rights as American-born, mother and child returned to our shores.

With them came fifteen rubberized packages of morphine, disguised as dirty diapers.

At that time morphine was worth $150 an ounce. It would be pleasant to state that Oriji's diapers were confiscated at the time the ship docked. Such, however, was not the case. The Customs inspector on duty was an experienced father and saw nothing unusual in the size of the baby's laundry bag. Mama Ogata first crossed our path when she made a sale to a peddler under surveillance by the Federal Narcotics Bureau.

The peddler, Chotaro Mintagowa, operated a cafe in Tacoma as a front for his more lucrative profession.

Mintagowa sold the morphine to a Narcotics Bureau Agent. He was arrested and eventually convicted and sent to jail. From him we learned that the leader of the ring was a Yokohama dealer named Shiraishi.

Polite and I talked it over.

"What next?"

"We could have Shiraishi arrested in Japan."

"He'd be found not guilty."

"Or be given a suspended sentence . . . ."

We weighed the alternatives. We were still speculating on our chances when the phone rang. It was Inspector Bernard Blonder of the California Division of Narcotics Enforcement.

Blonder had just picked up a Chinese in San Francisco.

"Thought you'd be interested. He's George King and he's done time in a Federal pen."

I remembered him. An old offender. "What's he done this time?"

"Well, he just carried a suitcase full of morphine off the Oakland ferry here. It's a fluffy type of stuff, nothing like what we usually pick up."

"Did you say it's fluffy?" I almost shouted into the phone.

The morphine Mrs. Ogata had brought ashore had been what we called "cotton" morphine. Possibly George's supply had been sent down from Seattle.

The connection proved even stronger when investigation showed that George King and Mrs. Ogata's husband had served time together in McNeil Island prison.

We decided to call on Mrs. Ogata. On a night in April she answered a knock at her door to find half a dozen Customs and Narcotics Bureau men gathered in the hall. There was nothing incriminating in her apartment, but she admitted she had left a suitcase with a neighbor. In the suitcase were seven bags of morphine—all that was left of her shipment.

Faced with the evidence, she confessed. She revealed that Shiraishi—already implicated by Mintagowa—had also served time at McNeil with Ogata. Upon release, Shiraishi had been deported.

We decided to keep Mrs. Ogata in custody, but to keep the news of her arrest secret.

Meanwhile we concentrated on George King who, unable to raise bail, abided gracelessly in jail. He refused to admit or confess anything.

"I don't want to go to prison again," he said wryly. "Maybe I be wise if I talk, help you catch others, so you be easy on me. But I take big chance getting my t'roat cut. So I follow Chinese proverb—'the foolish live long.' I be foolish —no speak nothing."

It was not our persuasion that wore him down finally, but a visit from his sweetheart—a cabaret dancer—who persuaded him that it was better to be a free man and take his chances on retribution than to stay in prison away from her.

So we came to an understanding. The government would postpone prosecution of George if he contributed information leading to the arrest of the ringleaders.

George, therefore, told us of another shipment of morphine that was expected.

"Seamen who bring stuff come coffee shop on Post Street. This time they not find me—I in jail," he complained.

We arranged his release by lowering the bail. He went to the coffee shop but came back to tell us that it was too late. Two Japanese seamen had already been there, failed to find him, and departed.

"They tell my boy at coffee shop they see me next time *Tatsuta Maru* come back. They say I got to have $3,500 ready," he reported.

We decided to set George up in style. We rented an apartment for him in San Francisco, furnished in gaudy Oriental fashion with fat little Buddhas all over the place, sitting on laquered, rickety tables. Hidden behind an elaborate imitation Ming vase was a dictograph. From it a wire ran to an adjoining apartment which had been rented by two of our men as a vantage point from which to listen in on George's visitors.

Every time a Japanese ship was in port, our men occupied this apartment. Whenever George made contact with one of the Nipponese, he phoned us and said something in Chinese—which we could barely understand. But the jargon was a signal that he was bringing a smuggler to the apartment. In addition to hearing the visitors talk, we wanted a chance to look at them. So we set up two mirrors—one in the hallway leading to George's apartment, the other inside the rooms occupied by our men.

By leaving the door to the hall open, our men in this way could see whoever went past, without themselves being seen.

All this led to many important arrests. One was made in New York, when George and I traveled across the continent to run down our smugglers.

On one occasion I even played the part of a stevedore to get some smuggled morphine off a ship and into the hands of our agents.

One day George received a letter from Japan which said that ten boxes of cocaine were being sent to him on a Japanese vessel. He was to have $5,000 ready. The ship was scheduled to leave Kobe around June 26th.

I checked the schedules and decided it must be the *Tatsuta Maru* again. She was due to sail for Japan on the 26th and make San Francisco on July 13th. But the *Tatsuta* arrived without incident. It was not until another ship, the *Nanman Maru* docked on July 19th that George received word there was someone waiting for him at the coffee shop.

The Chinese was worried about the $5,000 they wanted.

"It will be in a coat, hanging in your closet, when you get back to the apartment," I told him.

I did not actually have that much money to bait the trap. But $1,000 in small bills, with a fifty-dollar note on the outside, gave the appearance of much more.

We went next door and waited. A half-hour later, George appeared in company with a sinister-looking little Japanese wearing spectacles. We heard the guest express satisfaction with the set-up and the bankroll. The dope, he told George, was aboard ship; but he did not dare take it off because "the American Customs is too suspicious of Orientals these days." To which George replied as instructed:

"I know a white man who's a stevedore. He help us."

He meant me. We had planned this ruse to protect our informer, George.

Later, at a designated meeting place in the park, I met George and his Japanese friend. I was dressed in rough clothes, talked loudly and insisted that I be given a hundred dollars for my efforts. The Japanese—whose name was Yada—was pleased to learn that I was wearing a "smuggler's belt" under my clothes. The belt came from the Customs stock of seized equipment.

Early next morning I walked up the gangplank of the *Nanman Maru*, wearing my stevedore clothes. The guard had been tipped off to let me pass.

I walked through one passageway after another until, in the hissing steam atmosphere of the engine room, Yada grabbed my elbow.

"This way," he directed.

He opened a steel door, leading me into a dark compartment. A bag was thrust into my hand. I opened my clothes and stowed the bag into my smuggler's belt. A short time later I presented two rubberized silk packages to Blonder and Polite. We tested the stuff on the spot. Morphine!

I had to go back for more. When I returned with my second load, I gave them instructions as to how to reach the compartment.

"You'll find me in there with Yada. Put on a good act of arresting me as well as the Jap."

Yada was again thrusting a package into my outstretched hand when Polite's flashlight broke through the darkness. The Japanese wrenched his hand back and hurled the package against a bulkhead. It broke open, spilling white powder.

"It's a double-cross," I yelled, making a show of trying to get away. But Polite bagged me. Handcuffed to Yada, I was marched off to the captain of the vessel. As the *Nanman Maru* would be subject to a fine for having contraband aboard, the ship's master was shown the morphine as proof of violation.

When we leaving the ship, several stevedores were standing on the dock. One of them pointed to me and called out:

"I knew that fellow was a crook the first time I looked at 'im!"

Everything had worked perfectly. Yada later was sentenced to five years in the penitentiary. The entire stevedore crew had seen me treated as a criminal, so I was free to try similar masquerades in the future. But one thing was certain—George King was of no more use to us. The dope ring could hardly be expected to deal with him further, inasmuch as his latest ventures always led to arrests and seizures.

The big game—Shiraishi—stayed in Japan. But one day in Mrs. Ogata's mail, which we scrutinized, we found a letter obviously from her husband:

"Dear Mineko:

After reaching America, how are you? Has everything gone well? From April 10 to 15, around that time, Mr.
Osugi from *Tosei Maru* will call at your place. After talking,
hope you will arrange everything well. Please make cash
payment in exchange. Please treat him nice. After giving
this man money in exchange of the article, please wire your
husband. Please write everything that has gone by in detail
by mail later."

Cautiously, it was signed only "A Friend."

The *Tosei Maru* was delayed by engine trouble. She finally reached Seattle on May fifth. Agents were stationed at
Mrs. Ogata's home in Tacoma. As soon as the vessel docked,
other Agents looked up Mr. Osugi. His first name was Koko
and he was a fireman in the engine room. They did not talk
to him—only looked at him long enough to be able to recognize him later. They reported him to be "a powerful, rather
good-looking, easily recognizable Jap."

We watched. Osugi did not go ashore that day nor the
next. He was seen hanging around the ship's rail often, as if
studying the waterfront. On the second day we intercepted a
note to Mrs. Ogata.

Osugi's instructions were terse and simple. She was to
meet him the following day at five p.m., at a place marked on
a map of Seattle which he enclosed. If she came by auto she
was to tie a handkerchief to one of the car doors. If she
walked, she was to wave a handkerchief toward any Japanese who looked as if he might be a nautical engineer. Then
she was to wait until he made the first move.

Obviously Osugi had never seen Mrs. Ogata. We decided
that a reasonable facsimile would serve our purpose. We had
one made to order for the job—a Japanese-American girl
called Suki. So, at the appointed time, Suki drove to the pier
in a taxi driven by our Agent Dave Swift, who spoke fluent
Japanese. The girl tied a handkerchief coyly to one of the cab
doors.

Our fish rose to the bait. He got into the cab with Suki and Swift drove them away. There followed two days of cab-riding and negotiations. Osugi was clever. After Swift had piloted Suki to her rendezvous twice, Osugi told her sharply to "get another cab—this one hangs around here too much." So, although I spoke no Japanese, I was the driver the night Suki and a strange Japanese we had not seen before got into the taxi. He carried a suitcase.

"Driver," said Suki in English, "take us to the bus station at 8th Avenue and Stewart."

Instead, I drove them to the Federal office building. There I covered the man with a gun and ordered him out of the cab. Handcuffed, guarded, he was left in the detention room while Suki explained that we had still another errand.

"There was too much of the stuff for one suitcase, so Osugi is waiting at the bridge with the rest of the load."

This time we got the real driver of the cab, gave him back his uniform and explained the situation. He drove with Suki to the bridge while we followed in a Customs car. Osugi began loading the remaining dope—seven tins of opium—into the cab. We caught him in the act.

A few months later he and his accomplice, whose name was Takeda, were found guilty.

Takeda was given a two-year term. Osugi was sentenced to the penitentiary for ten years on one count, for one year on a second charge. Later, Federal Judge John Bowen changed the term to eleven years and one day. Osugi complained loudly at this. He figured an eleven-year term meant 4,015 days in jail, and he didn't want another day added on!

So Osugi went to McNeil Island. The Treasury Department, to prove how serious it considered the matter, fined the steamship line operating the *Tosei Maru* the sum of $12,790. The seized dope was worth nearly $50,000.

Mrs. Ogata, too, was convicted and sent to prison.

It looked as though we had scored a real victory.

Something else, however, came to light about Osugi.

Instead of being a fireman or a merchantman as he seemed to be, Osugi actually was a lieutenant commander in the Imperial Japanese Navy!

*   *   *   *   *   *   *   *

The discovery of Osugi's identity sent us off on another tack. By the time we had tracked down a few more of his assistants, the general pattern was beginning to emerge—sinister and clear, a new facet in the problem we had to face on the Pacific coast.

The Japanese narcotic smuggling syndicate was one single organization, from the Canadian line to the Mexican border. More than that, the profits all went to the American leader of the syndicate, to be expended in espionage.

I gathered these ominous facts together and wrote a long report to Washington.

The next week, a telegram summoned me to the nation's capital.

I went in some trepidation, not sure I had not made some mistake, wondering whether I had stepped too hard on Japanese toes, considering the currently uneasy state of United States relations with Japan. During my years in the Customs Bureau, I had made many trips to Washington, to give reports, to check on assignments, for conferences and —once or twice—for reprimands!

My boss, Thomas J. Gorman, put me at my ease almost at once. After the usual, "How're the crooks treating you, Mel?" he went straight to the point.

"You're here for a promotion—and to see the Secretary of the Treasury. We're establishing a special organization to fight the Japanese tooth and nail. An all-star team—and you're going to captain it."

Mr. Morgenthau was graciousness itself. He had, he said, read my reports concerning the Japanese organization.

He agreed with my conclusions. Because I knew the situation and because of the recommendations of my chiefs, he was choosing me for the new job he had in mind. In it, all the resources of the Treasury Department would be behind me. . . .

The Secretary then called in the heads of all his law enforcement groups: the chief of the Intelligence Unit of the Bureau of Internal Revenue, the chief of the Alcohol Tax Unit, the head of the Secret Service, the Commissioner of the Bureau of Narcotics, the Commandant of the Coast Guard, as well as the Commissioner of Customs.

Each was asked to notify his Pacific coast offices that I was especially representing the Secretary of the Treasury and that, until further orders, they were to give me any aid or personnel that I requested, without hesitation. Nor were they to ask why I made the request nor make any inquiries at all concerning it. Right or wrong, he told me, he would back me up. I should have every tool in the Treasury's chest to get the Japanese plotters. As a finale he added sternly, "And if I find out you needed something, Hanks, and didn't ask for it, or if you ask for it and let some bureaucrat bluff you out of it, I'll hold you responsible!"

A big order.

After the department heads left, we ironed out the many details. I was to make my reports directly to Harold Graves, Mr. Morgenthau's executive assistant, who would also keep him advised as to developments. Naval Intelligence had promised complete cooperation, also. He gave me a list of officers whom I could contact when the need arose.

When we parted, the Secretary shook my hand and said smilingly, "It looks like you're going to be a busy man for a long time, Mr. Hanks!"

That truly was an understatement. I started working on the new assignment during the train trip back home—so that the day after my arrival in Seattle, I was able to airmail to Mr. Graves a complete chart of my planned organization, with my reasons for believing it would get results. For security, I typed these notes myself at home.

Then I began to set up the organization as a working force. Before I was through I had over two hundred men working for the government, operating in three separate groups, each group thinking they were alone on the job.

We made good progress, as time went on. Less and less heroin and morphine were reaching this country, more and more Nipponese smugglers were taking a boat ride to McNeil Island penitentiary.

In the more secret and vital part of our task, we began also to move ahead.

I had an exceptionally good informer, a white man whom I shall call Earl. This man had lived in Japan for many years. He spoke the language and, more important, he knew Oriental thought and reaction.

From him we learned we were right in believing the Japanese narcotics organization to be backed by the Japanese government. He also confirmed our belief that the subsidized narcotics shipments were used to finance their espionage system in the United States.

And we learned still another thing—that the many Japanese gambling houses on the West Coast were tied in both with smuggling and spying.

A single syndicate, we discovered, owned and operated the entire string of these gambling houses, and the head of the organization was T. Sasaki, who lived in a country mansion near Milwaukee, Oregon, about ten miles outside of Portland.

This was verified by Earl. "You know," he said, "how the Japs act before a superior. Well, the first time you get a chance, watch how every one of the boys conducts himself when Sasaki's around. Even the Jap Consuls-General in Seattle and San Francisco kow-tow before him. I've seen 'em.

He's the biggest shot on the West Coast, probably an admiral or a major-general under orders to run this show."

T. Sasaki became our prime target from that moment. A lucky break came when the *Venice Maru* berthed in Seattle.

One of the Customs guards on duty at the pier was propositioned to allow a case of whisky to be taken ashore, to provide refreshments for a party the ship's officers were giving for some shore-side friends. If he would conveniently be blind, there would be another case of imported Scotch for him.

The guard reported the proposed bribe and was told by Agent Emerick to pretend to accept it. Agents were placed around the ship. That night, when not a case of whisky but a load of narcotics was brought ashore, they seized the contraband and tracked the smugglers to two expensive cars waiting on the beach. The agents were unable to arrest the drivers but they got the license numbers. A quick call to our Portland office disclosed the fact that both licenses had been issued to Sasaki.

Sasaki himself was at home in bed. Even had he not been, we could scarcely have charged him directly with the smuggling. Seattle, where the contraband was brought ashore, is over two hundred miles from Portland. However, we put on the heat, and evidently Sasaki took alarm, for suddenly, instead of answering questions which were likely to incriminate him, he sailed for Japan.

Sasaki's place was taken at once by a much more aggressive Oriental, Kanekichi Yamamoto. Our records showed that Yamamoto, small in size but large in arrogance, had been tried fourteen times for murder and acquitted each time—principally because the witnesses, all Japanese, had invariably disappeared or met with violence.

From Canada to Mexico there were forty-two gambling houses known in each city by the name of "Little Tokyo

Club." Their annual income was, at this time, approximately a million dollars. This sum was now at Yamamoto's disposal. We were sure, although we still had to prove it, that he was spending this money where it would do the United States the greatest harm.

Sasaki had been content to stay at home and issue orders. But Yamamoto had a restless foot. He traveled constantly up and down the coast. This enabled us to tie him in with several groups, including some Japanese fishermen whose boats were based on Terminal Island in the harbor of Los Angeles.

These fishermen, we learned, were foolishly charting every foot of the southern California coast. Foolishly, because they might have written Washington and, for a few cents, secured the best maps that could be drawn.

They also were camera addicts. Each fisherman took pictures of everything he saw. The reasons for some of these snapshots kept our men puzzled. Just what military use, for instance, might be made of a picture of pigeons in Los Angeles' Pershing Square? Is it even now somewhere mislabeled "Carrier Pigeons Being Exercised near Fort MacArthur"?

Another stroke of luck came to us. The *Heian Maru* had arrived at Seattle on one of her more or less lawful visits. We arranged for a special group of searchers to check the cargo and passengers. The merchandise consigned to a Portland suspect was checked first and found to be in order. But the agents decided to check all the cargo, even if that meant a week's hard labor.

Among the shipments were one hundred tubs of soy sauce. On close inspection the tubs were found to contain not only the sauce but to have special built-in containers, each of which held a large amount of morphine.

This shipment was traced to one of Yamamoto's lieutenants, Tensaka, who was arrested. A routine case, except for one extraordinary circumstance:

On board the *Heian Maru*, en route from Japan to England, was Prince Chichibu of the Japanese Royal Family. The fact that contraband drugs had been found on the same ship with a Prince of the Blood was, apparently, an insult to the Emperor.

Things began to happen.

Soon afterward, I received a letter from Graves, enclosing a photostat of another letter which our State Department had received from the Japanese government. This letter requested permission to send Inspector Shinji Taniguchi of the Japanese Imperial Police to visit the United States, that he might learn the identities of the Japanese narcotics laws violators. This information, in turn, the letter said, would provide him with leads as to the illicit shipping organizations in Nippon. And the Japanese police would be enabled to arrest the guilty persons. . . .

The Japanese actually had no desire to stop the enormously lucrative narcotic shipments. What they did want to know was how we were able to discover and confiscate so many of them. Since our new organization had been set up, few consignments had cleared port.

In his covering letter, Graves wrote that permission for the visit had been duly granted. He also named the steamer on which the Inspector would arrive. I was instructed to meet the visitor, be courteous, friendly, and keep him entertained. On the other hand I was to tell him nothing that would jeopardize our investigations or enable him to get a working knowledge of our set-up.

So I met Taniguchi at the dock. From the moment I held out my hand to take his in greeting until I waved farewell to him as his ship sailed out the Golden Gate, I stuck at his side. He proved to be a serious-minded and highly intelligent gentleman. As he could speak no English, one of our best interpreters, Willard Kingsbury, made a constant third to our party.

Taniguchi had the soul of a tourist. We visited all the points of interest on the Pacific coast—including the various penitentiaries and jails. He was especially interested in our treatment of prisoners. He had brought with him the fixed idea—which nothing could dispel—that inmates of our penal institutions were paid a salary of two dollars a day!

One Saturday afternoon we watched two teams of convicts play a hotly contested game of baseball, with the rest of their fellows rooting vociferously for their favorites and condemning the umpire in true American fashion. Taniguchi greatly enjoyed it. He was a real follower of the sport and could quote batting and pitching averages of Japanese players at length. Football, however, was strange to him. We attended a banquet in Seattle for the University of Washington football team. Before we left the table, Taniguchi had been sold on the sport.

Later, in Los Angeles, we took our visitor to see a game between Washington and the University of Southern California. Washington lost the game—and all through the losing contest the Inspector was depressed, his head hunched between his shoulders, his spectacles sliding forward on his nose. Then, Washington executed a brilliant forward pass. Suddenly my guest leaped to his feet, his cry ringing out over and above the rooting section:

"Banzai! Banzai!"

It was my turn to hunch my head between my shoulders. The looks we got from the spectators clearly showed that Californians had little love for the Japanese at that time.

I took Taniguchi to assorted places of amusement—ranging from the semi-cultural to the frankly risqué. He never laughed. Finally, during a visit to San Quentin, a trusty who had some wood carvings on display looked at Taniguchi's serious face and asked me if anything had amused him during his visit to this country.

"Nothing," I said. "Not even a movie comedy."

"The Japanese sense of humor," said the trusty, "is very different from the American. Wait—I'll show you."

He fumbled among his carvings and brought out one of an elephant balanced precariously on an egg. When the Inspector looked at it he laughed uproariously. He bought the carving as a cherished souvenir.

As best as I could I acted the considerate host, and always picked up the check despite his protests. He was unfailingly the interested and grateful guest—but all the time we were sparring, each trying to obtain useful information while revealing none.

I had asked Kingsbury to consider each word I said before translating any of my sentences so that nothing might be misunderstood.

Finally I began to get somewhere. Taniguchi at last asked me who I thought was the most notorious Japanese law violator in my district.

Yamamoto knew he was under constant investigation, so I had nothing to lose when I named him. Taniguchi considered this, then asked if I would like to talk to Yamamoto.

"No," I replied emphatically. "I don't want to do anything that might seem like asking a favor. But if Yamamoto wants to talk to me, I'll be glad to hear what he has to say."

Taniguchi pondered this for twenty-four hours. Then he instructed Kingsbury to tell me he was going to ask Yamamoto to fly down from Seattle for a conference in Los Angeles.

Two days later the king-pin smuggler called on me in my hotel room.

I had been notified in advance of the appointment, which gave me time to have Customs Agent Rae Vader and Special Agent Chase of the Internal Revenue Intelligence Unit there to meet him. (Vader later became Supervising Customs Agent at Los Angeles.)

I introduced Chase as another Customs Agent—hoping that Yamamoto, in attempting to deny and back away from charges of narcotic violations, would admit his gambling connections and so get involved with the income tax buzz-saw. We figured the Japanese knew that gambling of itself was not, at that time, a violation of Federal law. (This has since been changed.)

Yamamoto spoke English. "I have not," he said by way of opening the discussion, "violated any of the narcotic laws for over three years."

He knew, of course, about our statute of limitations!

Arrogantly, he went on to tell us that he was a loyal citizen of Japan and entirely uninterested in rendering assistance to United States law officers in any capacity whatsoever. He had come to Los Angeles only because Taniguchi had advised him that the Japanese government forbade any of its nationals any violations of the United States narcotics laws. Now that he knew this officially, he would immediately order his gambling house operators to have absolutely nothing to do with narcotics.

"And if my men disobey my orders," he declared, waving his hand in lordly manner, "you will not have to prosecute them, only bury them. You will find each violator in a sack—dead—before your office door in Seattle."

He shook hands with Taniguchi and stalked haughtily out the door.

After we had left Taniguchi, Vader and I talked it over with Chase. We were not in the least impressed with Yamamoto's promise to stop narcotic dealing, but we were delighted that he had so definitely admitted his connection with the gambling clubs.

It was Taniguchi's one contribution to our objective. He departed soon afterward for Japan—taking with him a trunkful of souvenirs, including the elephant carving—but carrying little information, at least nothing that would hamper our work.

Things happened often and fast after the Inspector's visit. Naturally Yamamoto did not keep his promise. Narcotics still came in, and my office hallway remained clear of corpses.

We also knew that, from all signs, war with Japan had come much closer.

One of these portents was an airmail, special delivery letter to Osugi, in prison, which we intercepted. It was signed "M. Endo" and the return address was Terminal Island, near Los Angeles. Translated, the letter advised that the writer had recently returned from a trip to New York where "some very successful work for the Emperor had been accomplished." It also referred to some highly confidential papers delivered to Endo by Osugi before the latter was imprisoned. Significantly, the writer inquired how long the steamship *Nitta Maru* would remain in Seattle, as Endo had "some documents for delivery in Japan."

Customs Agent A. D. Hansen and I traced M. Endo. We found her to be a Japanese woman employed in a restaurant run by Japanese and frequented by military officers from Fort MacArthur, as well as by Navy personnel from San Pedro and Long Beach. At that time we could do nothing but keep her under surveillance.

Later, when all Japanese nationals were removed from the state, she was sent to Utah.

Finally, Agent Vader secured an informer who knew all the details of the operation of the gambling clubs. He also was familiar with how and where the account books were kept—information vital to the government.

We decided to raid all forty-two gambling houses simultaneously.

Planning meticulously, we left nothing to chance. An Intelligence Unit Agent from the Internal Revenue Bureau, together with officers from every other Treasury unit, were in each raiding party.

On the night set for the raids, I was waiting tensely for the outcome.

I visualized the forty-two squads forming quietly at their various meeting places up and down the Pacific coast, poised for the crack-down.

As minutes went by, I kept looking at my watch, wondering whether anything had gone awry with our carefully-laid plans.

No reports yet. Maybe the Japanese had been forewarned.

Then the phone began to ring.

For several hours I answered one call after another. With enormous relief I learned the outcome.

The raids had succeeded—every one of the forty-two! The unit chiefs were jubilant.

Much documentary evidence was seized. Later, at the trial in Federal court, all the important members of the Japanese organization on the Pacific coast were convicted of income tax evasion.

After serving his sentence, Yamamoto was deported to Japan.

I learned later he went to Manchuria to supervise a large narcotics manufacturing plant operated by the Japanese. Still later, he was reported engaged in espionage work in the Dutch East Indies.

In a way, my job might have been considered finished. The closing of the gambling houses caused a scramble to name Yamamoto's successor in the racket. This scramble lasted until the removal of the Japanese from the coast after Pearl Harbor.

Much could be written about the intrigue, murders, kidnappings and accusations made during this period. But our primary interest was to forestall another powerful combine of gambling, narcotics and espionage—and in this we were successful.

Some Interesting Characters

ONE OF THE MOST ENGAGING
public enemies I ever met was Karl Beitzer, chief engineer
of the ill-fated ship *Marbella*. Elsewhere in this narrative I
write about Karl—who served us well as an informer during the months while he was waiting to appear as a witness
in the *Marbella* case.

Karl spoke excellent Japanese and we used him as an
undercover man in dealing with the smugglers. His great
usefulness lay partly in his appearance. Of German origin,
he was a slender, dapper man, blond and ascetic-looking.
Well-tailored clothes, plus a monocle, gave him entry into
law-abiding and law-dodging circles alike. Law-abiders
thought him dashing and cosmopolitan. Law-dodgers saw in
him a man obviously successful in his violations.

Beitzer always looked prosperous. Although he had no
money throughout his "stay" with us, except the three dollars a day we paid him for his informing activities, I never
saw him without his shoes polished and his mustache waxed.
His scanty wardrobe was always carefully pressed.

Women—all kinds—found him irresistible. Karl found
them equally so. It became Girard Polite's job, which occu-

pied most of his time, to keep Karl away from women so he could concentrate on his work for us. In this Girard was never entirely successful. There was always the landlady or the girl next door. Perhaps the secret of our Don Juan's charm was that he showed little discrimination!

Once we found it expedient to place Karl and Girard in a seaport town where a suspected smuggling gang could contact the German easily. We boarded Beitzer and Polite in a private home owned by a lone spinster whose strait-laced demeanor made even Karl shy.

I went there one morning and found Polite in the kitchen washing dishes.

"How did you get conned into this?"

Polite looked pained. "Because she leaves the egg on the plates when she washes them, and a ring inside the cream pitcher. It takes my appetite so I thought I'd clean them up while she's out."

In those days, breach of promise suits were frequent. Before Karl was finally deported, three of these suits had been filed against him by women in Seattle and Portland. He put the court summonses away as souvenirs, not in the least perturbed. He was going to be deported and he had no money, anyway, so how could they punish him? When he finally said goodbye to Polite and me, there were real tears in his eyes.

We regretted, somewhat, seeing him go. His talk about politics had interested us. Beitzer was a German who took very seriously his country's place in international affairs. It was from him, in the early thirties, that I learned about Adolf Hitler.

The last we heard of Karl, shortly before World War II, he was running a cafe in Canton, China—catering, of course, to the most exclusive international clientele.

What the fortunes of war did to him is uncertain. But

somehow, I cannot imagine Karl being liquidated. At least, not by Chinese Communists—whose firing squads, I understand, are sometimes made up of women.

❋ ❋ ❋ ❋ ❋ ❋ ❋

Captain Ypma, Karl's associate in the *Marbella* case, possessed an opposite personality trait. If Karl knew how to please people, Ypma as certainly knew how to antagonize them.

He was a sour little Dutchman in his late sixties—a hard, unleavened dumpling of a man. With Karl, our problem was to locate him where he would not become too popular. With Ypma, we had trouble finding a place where people would tolerate him at all.

We were not using the sea captain as an informer. But it was necessary to keep him hidden until the trial so that he would not be done away with. He had decided to plead guilty and testify for the government. At first, it was the racketeers we feared; after a while, it was Ypma's neighbors.

His fondness for seafood was his undoing. Fish was his favorite food and he liked it best dried. Moreover, he was convinced that he alone knew the proper procedure for curing this delicacy.

It was almost his sole subject of conversation. In a section of the country where fishing was a prime occupation and most families dried part of their own catch, we thought Ypma would feel at home.

But he brashly told them they were doing it all wrong. He constantly criticized their methods of drying their salmon and halibut. A few of the native residents agreed with the Dutchman. Arguments became violent and feuds smoldered.

Finally, to restore peace, we took him to another locality. This place was away from the water, in a neighborhood where fish was something to be bought at a market. But

Ypma continued to dry his fish as before. The smell of his partly-cured "crop" hung on the foggy air until the whole neighborhood rose up in rebellion.

We found a place for our problem captain at last, on an island near Vancouver, where he dried fish to his liking, while his neighbors, in stony silence, adhered to their own way. This time we had it figured right. The neighbors were Indians, and neither they nor the sea captain could understand each other's language.

❉ ❉ ❉ ❉ ❉ ❉ ❉

One night while Terry Tallent, an Agent of the Federal Narcotics Bureau, was standing weary guard with me outside Wong Toy's rented cabin, he said, as he poured a cup of coffee from a thermos: "If I ever change jobs, I think I'll be a ribbon clerk."

He drank his coffee, not taking his eyes off the cabin.

Wong Toy was a little grey Chinese who looked slightly like a drawing of Confucius. Before we finally cornered him he gave us a lengthy chase.

In small precise ways, he made use of ingenuity equal to that of the smartest of international smugglers. In small precise doses, weighed out in dime store envelopes, he distributed enough pure heroin to stock a chain of drug stores.

Wong drove two cars. One, a conservative sedan, he used for ordinary business purposes. It stood outside his house most of the time, although on rainy days he usually drove it into a vine-covered carport on the side of his house.

The other car was an inconspicuous coupe. He parked it at a distance from his home, at different times and places. The wily little man never approached this car directly but went to it circuitously by heading in the opposite direction.

Circling the block, Wong Toy would take careful notice. When he was satisfied no one was near, he would get into the car and slowly start off. He never carried anything to or from this car. When he was not in it, we checked it several times and found nothing. So we knew we would have to follow him on one of his trips.

He had a trick that made tailing difficult. He had timed the traffic signal lights so exactly that he knew to the very second when to cross, leaving any car following him facing the red light. If we followed, we ran through the red signal, which showed him we were after him. In this case, he would drive around the block and go home. On the other hand, if we waited for the light to turn green, he almost always got away from us on the first signal. If not, he evaded us for certain on the second or third.

But one night we picked him up on a road outside of town.

Staying a quarter of a mile behind him, we saw him turn into a driveway leading to a group of beach cottages, apparently to sleep, since all lights were turned off within a few minutes.

At two-thirty, however, as if on signal, the lights came on again. We thought this might reveal something. Apparently the Chinese was trying to make contact with somebody. But nothing happened. The lights went off again and all was quiet.

Tallent and I, after a sleepless vigil, went to our offices and yawned through our work. We caught a few hours of sleep in the late afternoon, but at dusk we were on our way to the cottage again, waiting for Wong.

He drove up and went through the same maneuvers. Again the lights, turned on at two-thirty in the morning, failed to produce a response. This went on for three nights. Then we got some excitement but not in the way we had expected. Shortly after three o'clock, a car drove up and a sheriff and two deputies went in to raid the place.

The proprietor of the cottages, noting the odd behavior of his guest, had decided he was a bootlegger.

All that we learned from the ensuing commotion was that Wong Toy had nothing concealed in his room. No liquor, no dope, not even a gun. The sheriff and his men went back empty-handed. Tallent and I stayed hidden and kept watching.

The next night when our suspect turned on his lights, he evidently received an answering signal. Almost at once he turned them off, opened the door, and walked briskly into the night.

At a safe distance we followed him down the road to the highway and on to a crossroad. We dared not come too close for fear he would hear our footsteps on the gravel. Watching with our glasses, we saw that he went toward an old farmhouse with a barn set far back from the road and surrounded by a cornfield. Wong entered the barn, stayed there for a while, then returned to the highway where he had left his car. We followed him back to the cabin—and then, when he settled down again, we caught a few hours of rest ourselves in the car.

The following night we trailed him again. Once more he entered the barn. At the same time two other men came out of the woods behind the barn and went in by another door. We immediately rushed in, arrested all three, and then reaped the reward for our nights of waiting.

Stuffed into corners, piled in boxes, packed into milk cans, and otherwise concealed from the casual eye were thousands of dollars worth of narcotics.

The man and woman who lived on the farm proved to be innocent. They had been hired by Wong Toy to keep the place and to provide meals for the men who came and went so mysteriously. Since it was during the depression and jobs were hard to come by, the white couple had accepted their pay and asked no questions of Wong Toy.

We hauled the men down to the Customs office. Here we

told our grey-bearded Confucius that he could telephone his family. Then, while Tallent watched him, I listened from the extension in the next room.

I don't know what we expected him to say, or what we thought the person on the other end of the wire would answer. But we were not prepared for the startling, brief communication that followed:

"Hullo," said the voice of what might have been Wong's Number One Son.

"I go jail now," said Wong abruptly, with a mournful inflection.

Then he hung up the phone. Just before the connection was cut, I heard Number One Son answer without surprise, "Hokay."

✿   ✿   ✿   ✿   ✿   ✿   ✿

Of all our informers, the most successful and most suave—if one can be suave and brash at the same time—was a fellow called Henry.

He lived on the West Coast and all through the years of Prohibition he represented Canadian distilleries interested in distributing their products through rum runners in this country.

Henry did well until the United States repudiated the Eighteenth Amendment. Then the distilleries decided to open a legal import business. They had no more use for Henry or Henry's connections. His bank account began to dwindle.

He was a dejected man until the day Customs Agent Emerick offered him a chance to recoup his finances.

Emerick explained that the Canadian distilleries which Henry had formerly represented could not yet do business in the United States. Our government had decided that, first, they must pay the duties and penalties involved on all the liquor they had been responsible for dumping into this country during Prohibition.

"Help us get the information we need and bring in the necessary witnesses, and you can get an informer's share of the collections," Emerick told him.

Henry did a few minutes' summing up in his head and then acknowledged that a possible share of several million dollars was worth a slight case of betrayal. Accordingly, he set about rounding up his former associates. As a number of these people were habitually at odds with the law, this took some doing and much time.

Eventually the United States government collected millions from Canadian liquor interests. Henry's share of this was almost $100,000. Out of this amount he was obligated to pay off his own informers.

But Henry disappeared. A few days later the informers descended on the Customs office with blood in their eyes.

"Where's our money?"

Emerick told them: "I'll get Henry back and see if he had anything left."

He sent out word that the Customs office wanted to see Henry.

Every day the unpaid informers came in to see whether we had located their man. They waited day after day.

A week later, Henry strode blithely into our office and announced he was again ready for "action".

"You'll get it," we told him. "Your unpaid helpers are waiting in the next room."

When we explained what had happened and that he would have to hand over the money, Henry's brow wrinkled.

"But I haven't got it. After all, that was ten days ago, and it was only a hundred grand!"

Then, apparently unworried, he said, "I want to talk to those men alone."

We had already searched the men for weapons. They had none. But they had fists to strike with and feet to kick with, and there were half a dozen of them to Henry's rather ineffectual one.

We let him go in, and listened outside for sounds of the violence we expected to have to stop.

No noise nor fighting was heard.

Our informer had not been a salesman most of his life for nothing. In about twenty minutes he came out smiling, his hand clutching a neat packet of hundred-dollar bills.

We looked at him in astonishment.

"I have explained the situation," he told us. "My friends were sorry for my predicament and have loaned me a little money."

Some months later, I was called to Washington for a conference. The newspapers were then running stories about a case which I had assisted in developing.

Apparently, Henry by chance was in the nation's capital at the time and had read the stories, because the next day he called at my hotel.

He was as friendly and amiable as ever. One would have thought we were fellow club members of long standing.

"I've come to show you around," he exclaimed.

Since I had seen Washington many times over, I made an excuse. But Henry was so insistent that I finally agreed to let him take me as far as the Customs office.

When we got outside, I realized why he wanted me to come with him. He had bought the longest, shiniest sedan I had ever seen. A uniformed chauffeur sat behind the wheel.

I looked at Henry in surprise. He said with pride, "I've done all right since I come back East."

It was after World War II when I met him again. I was then in the Customs office in Los Angeles when someone brought in word of a fellow who ostensibly was selling neckties near the harbor, but was suspected of exporting an illegal commodity.

Doubtfully, I went down to the docks with the Agent-in-Charge.

It was Henry. As we got there he opened a box of samples and began handing out the neckties.

When he saw me, he smiled expansively.

"Mel Hanks! What a lucky surprise! Let me give you a tie—here's the very thing for you—"

I refused it with thanks.

As far as we could determine, he was working at a perfectly legal occupation, with no chance that someone could turn the tables and inform on him.

Strayed Contraband

Even the cleverest methods of dropping contraband over the side from inbound vessels are prone to error. At times, some of the unlawful booty unquestionably was lost. We Customs men often wondered what happened to the loads the smugglers failed to retrieve from the water promptly.

The result of one such smuggling failure was revealed to us by accident.

Our Agent in Japan had reported to us in March, 1937, that a large consignment of morphine was en route to Seattle on a particular ship. He also told us that, on this vessel's last voyage, the cook had thrown ten pounds of that drug down the garbage chute off Point No-Point, where pick-up men in a small rowboat had safety caught it.

Point No-Point is at the narrowest spot on the shipping lane between the Straits of San Juan de Fuca and Seattle. On it at that time were several small boat-houses whose owners rented rowboats and outboard motors to amateur fishermen.

So it seemed logical that another dumping would be tried at that same spot. Immediately after receiving the information, we started shadowing those places in Seattle's

Japanese settlement which suspects might ordinarily visit.

On the tenth day we were rewarded. Three Japanese with a Los Angeles license plate on their car checked into a hotel. This particular hotel was operated by Japanese and patronized exclusively by them. The inn was not above suspicion—in fact, it figured in the files of most of the local law enforcement agencies.

We centered our attentions on its newest guests. By rotating our cars, we kept the place under continuous surveillance. When the three men we were watching drove to a boat-house one day two miles below Point No-Point, we followed. Through field glasses we saw them hire a rowboat with outboard motor and fishing tackle. They returned to the hotel without going out in the boat.

The day that the ship named by our Tokyo Agent was due to dock was one of rain and wind. Nevertheless the three suspects drove to the boat-house and waited. About mid-afternoon, Polite, Ballinger and I saw them rowing out into the Sound with their fishing equipment.

This was significant. Salmon do not strike in heavy, rough seas. True fishermen would have waited until the weather cleared.

We parked our car where it would not be seen, and climbed a cliff above the beach. Here we could watch both the incoming ship and the men in the boat.

Half an hour later the ship came abreast of our lookout. The March afternoon was short and the sky cloudy, but we still could see the vessel. We held the glasses tightly to our eyes, impatiently wiping the fogged-up lenses.

The trio lowered their poles and lifted their caps in unison, as if in signal to someone on the ship. A moment later we saw a heavy splash just aft the stern.

The contraband evidently had been dropped.

At this time the supposed fishermen were half a mile

from the spot. They immediately dropped their pretense of angling, started the motor and sped toward the booty.

At that moment, the weather penalized the boatmen. A violent sea churned up and the next instant the whole area was blotted out by a raging squall. The rain rushed down in sheets, the wind became a gale, and towering waves threatened to swamp the small rowboat.

Our glasses were useless. We could barely see each other. We could only huddle in our dripping raincoats until the storm passed. Staring at the spot where the contraband went overboard, we could see only rough, gray water.

Then Polite gave a shout and pointed to an object about a quarter of a mile offshore. There was the rowboat. Evidently the motor had stalled, for two of the occupants were paddling while the third bailed water. We had no way of knowing whether or not they had picked up anything, but we believed they had not. This was confirmed when they reached the shore for, although it was nearly dark, we could see that they carried no packages.

Their failure was obvious when, instead of returning to Seattle, they rented a cabin nearby and settled down for the night. After they apparently were asleep, we rented another cabin nearby and set up hourly watches.

At five a.m., when Ballinger had the watch, he roused us to report that it would be high tide in half an hour.

High tide can be a great bonanza for Customs men. At that time smuggled narcotics might be cast up on the beach. Drowsily we got up. The three Japanese also had risen and were on their way down to the shore.

We followed cautiously. It was not yet fully daylight but we could see the flashlights they carried. Watching from behind hummocks, we saw the three searchers slowly walking up and down the beach, minutely inspecting every object washed up by the tide.

It was evident that they had no success. They returned to their cabin to wait for the next high tide.

This game of waiting and looking continued for three days and nights. During all this time the seas were too high to launch a boat and search offshore.

Finally they gave up. We followed them back to Seattle and kept them under observation until they crossed the Washington-Oregon state line on their way south.

As far as the Japanese were concerned, that smuggling attempt was a loss. A week later, however, Agents Atherton, Bradt, Polite and I were sitting at the counter of a drug store across the street from our office when the lost shipment of contraband dramatically came alive.

An uncouth, dull-looking boy of about eighteen, dressed in jeans and a leather jacket, walked in. He would hardly have been noticed except that he carried such a strong odor of the barnyard that he attracted our attention even before we heard him ask for the manager.

The proprietor was a friend of ours, so we knew he did not mind if we overheard the conversation.

To our complete astonishment we heard the boy ask him, "Mister, do you want to buy some dope?"

Involuntarily the manager glanced our way. Our rapt attention must have convinced him that we were pulling a gag on him, and he decided to go along with it.

"Sure," he said. "I'm always in the market for dope if the price is right."

Then, in a loud whisper, clearly for our ears, he demanded:

"Where's it hidden?"

The boy looked puzzled. "It's right here."

From inside his jacket he pulled out an oblong can and opened it. It was filled with pure morphine!

Despite his amazement—and ours—the druggist

thought quickly. Although the youth was clearly an amateur, he still was trying to peddle dope—most likely smuggled—and that made it a case for Customs.

In a loud voice so we could hear, the druggist said: "This is morphine, all right, but I can't use this much. Maybe these guys at the counter might go in on the deal. They're a slick bunch. Go ask them."

The boy brought the can over for our inspection. We told him to come with us. Our druggist friend came along, too. We went to our office and, while the kid sat numbly staring at our door where the words "U.S. Customs" stood out, we examined the can. It was wrapped in the typical waterproofed silk used by the Japanese narcotics factories.

"How did you get this?" we asked.

Too frightened to lie, the boy told us about it.

His name was Tom Blank. He lived on a dairy farm operated by his father, Jerry Blank, on the southern end of an island directly across the Sound from Point No-Point. The week before, Tom said, he had been giving his dog a run along the beach when the animal stopped to sniff a strange-looking package cast up by the tide. Examination showed this to be several large slabs of cork done up in canvas. Inside were two large, heavy cans—too well soldered for him to open with his pocket knife.

He took his find home. His father helped him pry open the cans. Inside each were smaller cans, with the spaces between stuffed with coarse, unbleached flour. The inner cans were filled with a powder different from anything they had ever seen or smelled.

Like all the residents of the area, they had heard many stories of smuggling. They had jumped to the correct conclusion at once—that this powder was some kind of narcotic and, as such, was worth a fortune if they could contact the proper buyers.

They knew, of course, that rightfully they should have brought their find to our office or to some other government agency.

After finding a hiding place for the loot, Jerry sent Tom to Seattle to try to peddle one of the smaller cans.

"Didn't you know it was illegal to sell it?" we asked him at this point.

The boy's face reddened. "Sure, I knowed it. But we don't have no money, and we figgered we'd take a chance. We knowed we had to sell it in the underworld, like the movies say. So I come down Main Street—"

We tried not to laugh as we listened to the incredible tale of this naive wayfarer on the path of iniquity.

He had first gone into a shooting gallery—a place run by a fellow named Rudy.

"I thought I's on the right track, but he turned me down. He said it was plaster o' paris and for me to go fly a kite."

"What did you ask him for that canful?" I questioned.

"Eighty dollars."

At that time, morphine sold for $350 an ounce, wholesale. That made his pound worth around $5,600. No wonder Tom had been turned down! No one in the racket could believe that genuine morphine would be available at that pittance.

"So I looked 'round and decided to try a drug store. My Dad buys medicine for our sick cows there, so I figgered I'd ask," he added ruefully.

We sat staring at him. What a picture he gave us! A big, dumb kid, wandering casually down one of Seattle's toughest streets with a small fortune in dope under his arm —yet neither robbed nor harmed!

Had any illicit dealers guessed what was in the package Tom carried, he almost certainly would have been slugged and robbed. And he would have been forced to admit that more narcotics were hidden at his father's farm, thereby possibly endangering his father's life.

With our entire searching crew, we took the boy and drove at once to the island via the ferry.

Jerry, the father, proved to be belligerent. He refused to surrender the morphine voluntarily. He saw a fortune being filched from under his nose—his plans, perhaps, for a new car, a motor boat, an electric milking machine—frustrated by Federal agents who drank their coffee at the wrong drugstore counter.

"How come you nosy guys loaf around like that?" Jerry asked angrily.

There was no question as to what must be done. But I felt some sympathy for him.

We had sufficient cause to search legally without waiting to secure a warrant, so we went to work.

It took us an entire day to get all of it. Some was hidden in milk bottles, some on beams in the barn, more in milk cans buried in the ground which we were able to locate by the freshly-spaded earth. Some also was in paper boxes—in an old rusty stove—and the rest buried in the fodder in the stable.

Of course we placed both father and son under arrest. At their attorney's advice, they pleaded guilty and received suspended sentences.

An Oriental Diplomat

THE BRITISH CUSTOMS AND EX-
cise officer beckoned to me as I entered his Hong Kong office.

In contrast to his usual suave complacency, my friend
seemed agitated as I sat down and asked, "Anything new?"

"My informer has brought me something that could
start international fireworks or get you transferred to Devil's Island," he replied.

Then he called in the Oriental informer who had been
waiting in a back room out of sight.

In foreign countries, liaison and mutual cooperation between U.S. Treasury men assigned there and the local government officials is a necessity. In Hong Kong the British Customs and Excise officers were always accommodating.

The informer advised that one of the big shippers of
narcotics had recently sold a large amount of morphine, heroin and smoking opium to a Mr. Ying Kow, of Washington,
D.C.

Inquiry revealed that Mr. Ying Kow was attached to
the staff of the Chinese ambassador to the United States.
This meant, of course, that he, his entourage and baggage
had diplomatic immunity from search by Customs upon arrival in the United States.

Such a situation was an extremely touchy one. Our own State Department in similar cases previously had always gone into a high fever and a condition of jitters. They objected to the mere mention of Customs searching diplomatic baggage.

The Customs Bureau would always back its agents to the limit with the proviso: "You have to be right." No margin of error was allowed in such cases as violating diplomatic immunity from search.

We Treasury investigators knew that if we made a positive allegation of smuggling in a specific case involving a foreign diplomat assigned to the United States, and that charge proved erroneous, our future prospects in the service, if we were permitted to remain at all, would be extremely dismal.

The situation obviously had to be handled with the utmost care.

"This is the type of thing that gives us nightmares," I told the British officer.

My presence in China at this time was on an investigation of alleged smuggling of narcotics from Macao to Honolulu. When I had obtained the information necessary for that case, I got passage aboard an American President liner and departed for Honolulu.

Before I boarded the ship, however, arrangements were made with my British friends in the Hong Kong Customs office to keep in close touch with the Ying Kow group. By radiogram or cable, in a special code we devised, they would notify me when the Chinese diplomat departed Hong Kong, the means of transportation and the destination.

Between concern over the Honolulu case and worry over the prospects involved in the Ying Kow matter, I had a restless voyage. Anxiety replaced sleep.

Would the Ying Kow group return via Hawaii to the

mainland United States, which was the usual route at that time, or would they go directly to the mainland?

If they proceeded via Hawaii, there would be a better chance to learn more about their baggage.

Customs has the lawful right to search and inspect any vessel or its cargo or baggage when in an American port. Before putting my neck on the block and advising Washington, I needed to know positively that the Ying Kows' baggage contained contraband.

If they went directly to the mainland, where their baggage would be officially passed, I debated what to do then. Merely pass the buck to one of my brother agents in whatever port they debarked and leave it up to him, or take the responsibility myself?

I disliked the thought of passing the buck to someone else. I also remembered that I valued my job, assignment and associates, and did not want to be sent into "exile".

Upon arrival in Honolulu I became so engrossed with the U.S. attorney in matters pertaining to the case then being prosecuted in Federal court there that my worries about the Ying Kow matter became submerged.

Finally, one morning during the height of the Honolulu trial, I received a radiogram in code from my British Customs friend in Hong Kong. The decoded message advised that the Ying Kow group of diplomats had left Hong Kong aboard a Japanese passenger vessel en route to San Francisco via Honolulu.

This information was most welcome because it gave us approximately two weeks to prepare our reception of the Ying group in Hawaii. It would take the Japanese ship about that long to reach Honolulu.

I told my troubles to the U.S. attorney who, of course, was as interested as myself in taking action. He arranged for a prominent Chinese friend of his to entertain Ying Kow and his party while in Honolulu. This was planned to keep the group away from the ship long enough to permit us to make a secret search of some of their effects.

While they were being so entertained we learned they had forty-seven trunks in the baggage room of the vessel. We managed to open one which was found to be loaded with narcotics. We closed it again, hoping that no sign of tampering was evident.

It was decided that, due to the fact the ship was a foreign one and that the passengers were not disembarking in Hawaii, the Ying Kows and also the trunks would be allowed to go on to San Francisco. The U.S. attorney immediately wired the Attorney General of the facts, and I informed the Customs Bureau in Washington.

Due to my propensity for worry, I thought of the possibility of the contraband being removed from the baggage prior to arrival in San Francisco and smuggled in by some other of many possible methods.

The Ying Kows' baggage was duly searched in San Francisco by Customs when the ship arrived. All forty-seven trunks were found to contain an immense shipment of heroin and morphine.

Both Mr. Ying Kow and Suzi Ying Kow, his wife, became, predictably, extremely angry, and in good English threatened the Customs officers with dire reprisals. They demanded the immediate presence of the Chinese Consul in San Francisco. When he arrived they ordered him, in excited Chinese, to contact the Chinese embassy in Washington and obtain their instant personal release, as well as that of their baggage.

Nevertheless, their pleas were ignored and we lodged them in the county jail. Within hours the State Department queried the Customs Bureau in Washington.

They asked whether narcotics had actually been found

in the Yings' baggage. After the Bureau assured them that a huge amount of contraband had been discovered, no more was heard from the State Department.

The Ying Kows were convicted in U.S. courts and given long sentences. Upon the request of the Chinese government, however, they were allowed to return to China.

A Lazy Third Mate

ONE SMUGGLING TECHNIQUE WE WERE trying doggedly to solve was employed by a benign, scholarly-appearing old Chinese who operated an importing firm on Grant Avenue in San Francisco.

We were positive he was importing narcotics in addition to his many legal commodities. We knew this because for a long time he had been sending large amounts of money by telegraphic transfer to the cable address of one of the largest shippers of illicit drugs in Macao. Then, too, it seemed that shortly after one of his legal importations had passed through Customs, the price of illicit narcotics went down, while at the same time the supply on the illegal market increased. This we learned from Federal and State narcotics agents.

We had searched very carefully, we thought, every one of the old man's shipments without finding anything questionable. He did a big business in selling live turtles, a rather small Oriental variety, all over California. But these were in open wooden tubs. We knew definitely it would be impossible to secrete any important amount of drugs in live turtles.

Then one morning we went down to board the SS *President Jefferson* to check into a shipment of merchandise which was arriving for our Chinese importer.

As we reached the Captain's cabin to make the routine announcement of our impending search, he opened the door and came out, followed closely by the Third Mate.

"This officer thinks he's found something you'd like to see," he greeted us.

The other man quickly spoke up:

"I want you men to see these tubs up here on deck. They look phony to me. Let me show you."

We followed as he almost ran toward the stern of the ship. There sat the usual shipment of twenty tubs of live turtles consigned to our suspect.

Pointing to one tub set apart from the others, the Mate said excitedly:

"I tried to bore through that one but the drill broke off like it hit metal. Must be a funny kind of tub."

Before delivery to the consignee, the steamship company regularly changed the water in the tubs. The usual way had been to take out the turtles, turn the tubs over, allowing the water to drain out, put the tubs back upright, fill them with fresh water and replace the turtles.

But this Third Mate, who was new to the ship, thought it would be much easier to bore holes in the bottom of a stave and let the water run out without removing the swimming occupants, thus eliminating a lot of work.

As he attempted to make the first hole, he hit metal. This proved to be a thin, long, narrow can of unusual size containing morphine.

The staves were of such size that the usual can containing narcotics could not possibly have fitted into the wooden stave. But the smuggler had special cans made to fit. This twenty tubs of live turtles produced forty pounds of heroin and morphine.

This was one of the few times that we had discovered contraband through sheer chance.

So our benign old Chinese, together with three associates, served the next five years as cooks and laundrymen at McNeil Island Federal prison.

Japanese Sampans

"WHITE STUFF AND MUD COMING in from Hawaii—trunk loads—big lot. No one here know the shipper but it's true for a fact."

The Chinese telling me this sat in my San Francisco office in the early thirties. He was an informer.

His appearance was that of a prosperous business or professional man—well-dressed, intelligent, and speaking passable English.

This informer had proved in the past to be reliable. I knew that "white stuff" meant morphine or heroin, and "mud" meant smoking opium. But I also knew that no narcotic-producing plants or shrubs were being grown in Hawaii. Thus I was inclined to be skeptical.

In any law enforcing activity there are always the informers. The important and very necessary function of any law enforcement agency is to be able to separate the genuine information from the false. This requires long experience and many disheartening efforts before one can acquire the ability to detect the real from the false. Even then mistakes are often made.

We of the Customs Agency Service, responsible for investigation of many Federal law violations, always tried to determine an informer's motive. It might be revenge, desire for money, or to divert us to one matter while he pulled a violation in some other locality himself. Often he was trying to eliminate a competitor. An informer's methods could be devious, but it was always important to determine his motive, if possible.

In spite of my skepticism, I remembered this informer's productive information in the past and realized that his insistence as to the contraband from Hawaii ought not to be entirely ignored.

Shortly afterward, I went to Hong Kong on another matter. While there, through the usual friendly cooperation with the British Customs, I checked arrivals of telegraphic transfers of money to the cable addresses of the principal narcotics shippers at Macao. These messages necessarily went through Hong Kong.

I discovered several transfers of large amounts of money from a cable address in Honolulu to a big narcotics wholesaler in Macao. The amounts of money involved in each instance were so large that it precluded any possibility that it paid for only a local supply in Hawaii. So there it was!

This brought to mind the informer in San Francisco. But why use the Hawaiian Islands for transactions that risked double jeopardy? The contraband had to be smuggled into Honolulu first, then a second hazardous transfer attempted to get it inside the mainland.

After careful thought, the idea did not seem so foolish after all. For example, if someone had developed what he thought was a fool-proof smuggling technique into the Hawaiian Islands, it might be a simple matter to get it from there to the mainland.

As long as the smuggler did not enter into any local distribution in the Islands, he would not run into competition with other racketeers and consequently would not become known. Once the narcotics were safely ashore in Hawaii, it was purely a domestic transaction. Sending it on to the mainland would be merely moving the contraband from one part of the United States to another. Baggage and merchandise from Honolulu were not ordinarily subject to Customs examination when they arrived at any mainland port.

The more thought I gave it, the clearer the plan became. It certainly would confuse the competition selling wholesale in the mainland United States, besides diminishing the likelihood of being caught.

After getting the cable address of the sender of the money from Honolulu, it was comparatively easy to determine his identity on my return. He proved to be a Chinese named Hong Suey. Due to the fact that I was fairly well known in Hawaii as a Federal officer, I arranged for two Customs Agents unknown there to maintain surveillance over the suspect and report to me.

Within a month the agents had established that the owner of two large sea-going Japanese fishing sampans was the suspect, Hong Suey. These sampans were operated for their boss by Japanese fishermen. After another month, the agents had determined the identity of three white Americans who were also working for Hong Suey. As passengers on steamers bound for the mainland, they apparently were taking trunk loads of contraband as baggage. Evidently this was for delivery to wholesale dealers of narcotics there.

At this point I went to Washington to confer with my superiors in the Bureau concerning the further development of this case. It was decided to attempt to make the seizure of the first and second loads of contraband, upon delivery at its final destination on the mainland, appear to be accidental, and not because of any prior knowledge. We knew that this might be difficult but we wished to protect our Honolulu set-up until we had pinpointed all members of the syndicate, including Hong Suey, the sampan crews, delivery men, and the wholesale purchaser himself, if possible.

We secured the assignment of several additional officers to assist in the shadow work necessary to achieve our objective.

Upon departure of the first trunk load of contraband, after we had completed our plans, both the carrier and the trunk were covered by one of our men from Honolulu to San Francisco. There the carrier and his trunk were kept under surveillance by several agents until departure for Tacoma, Washington. Two other agents accompanied the suspect to Tacoma where our men from the Seattle main office took over. They successfully seized the trunk load of contraband and arrested both the carrier and the consignee. It was not necessary to use the agents especially assigned for shadow detail, so we could continue to use them on the next trip. The Seattle agents made it appear as though they were acting on local information when they made the seizure and the double arrests.

These events started a conflict between two smuggling organizations in Tacoma and Seattle. One group immediately was convinced they had been informed on by the other. Our Seattle office was able to take advantage of the "war" and make several more seizures and arrests.

The way things worked out in Tacoma left our Hawaii shippers unsuspicious. They fully believed they had lost their trunk load of contraband and one of their carriers had been arrested because of an apparent squabble between two Northwest syndicates.

It wasn't long before our agents assigned to the shadow detail advised us that the second carrier had bought a ticket from Honolulu to San Francisco on a streamer.

One of our special detail agents accompanied the carrier and his trunk. Upon arrival in San Francisco the surveillance was taken over by two agents there who shadowed the carrier and his trunk when he departed for Los Angeles. At that city Los Angeles agents took over and were successful in seizing the trunk load of narcotics and arresting both the carrier and the Los Angeles customer.

In spite of these successes, we became concerned now, fearing that this would be too much for the Honolulu syndicate to take without folding up prematurely. Surprisingly, though, within a month, the third and last carrier known to us bought a ticket to San Francisco.

As before, one of our shadow agents accompanied this third carrier with his trunk of narcotics to the mainland. It soon became apparent that this load was for local delivery. Luck was still with us, however, because our San Francisco agents were able to seize the carrier, the trunk and the consignee.

This, we knew, would end the case. Three "knockovers" in succession would be too much for the racketeers. In the meantime we had gotten secret indictments in Honolulu against all participants there, and were enabled to arrest Hong Suey and members of the crew of the Japanese fishing sampans.

The Japanese were rather small fry, but confessed to their part in the conspiracy. They also revealed to us something we had not previously known.

It was the method used to smuggle the contraband into Hawaii. Obeying instructions from Hong Suey, they had met Japanese freighters hundreds of miles at sea and, by pre-arrangement, had picked up packages thrown overboard from the ships. On the way back to Honolulu, they always made their usual catch of fish, but turned over the contraband to Hong Suey.

All defendants pleaded guilty and received sentences to Federal penitentiaries. We were gratified with the guilty pleas because this meant we did not have to disclose the identity of any of our shadow agents, and thus could use them again if necessary in the Hawaiian Islands or elsewhere.

Paneled Walls

CHINESE FAMILY CLANS OR tongs are among the most loyal in the world. Even Mao Tse Tung's "cultural revolution" has failed to break up these family groups which have held together for countless generations.

This family loyalty was manipulated by several syndicates for smuggling while the American President Line was using Chinese as room boys and waiters on vessels operating between the Orient and United States ports on the Pacific coast.

The system of hiring Chinese employees by steamship lines was to hire all their Oriental personnel through a Chinese shipping agent. In typical Chinese style, this meant that the hiring agent would place on one particular ship only members of the same family clan or tong. This insured harmony among the crew, but made it difficult for Customs officers because no member of a Chinese family tong would inform on any other member of that same clan. All Chinese crew members were under the immediate direction of a Chinese usually referred to as the comprador or "Number One Boy."

The design used by the narcotic syndicate associated

with a particular crew was to place one of their carriers aboard at Hong Kong on any President liner bound for U.S. Pacific coast ports via Shanghai. The carrier always traveled first class, chiefly because of the ornate paneling in first class cabins.

The contraband carried in luggage would be hidden behind the paneled walls of the stateroom occupied by the syndicate carrier. This was usually done by one of the crew members who was employed for his expertness with paneling work.

When Shanghai was reached, the syndicate passenger was at the end of his voyage. A new passenger, entirely innocent and unaware of the smuggling venture, would be assigned this room for the remainder of the trip to the United States.

The Chinese crew members were well aware that Customs searching squad would not wreck the paneling of staterooms unless in possession of definite information that one particular room contained contraband.

Various methods were used to get the contraband ashore once the vessel was in an American port. One of the most successful techniques was for the Chinese crew members to wait until all passengers and cargo had been discharged from the ship. Then, on the night before departure, the contraband would be taken out by the crew member who was the expert in panel work. It was then packed in weighted, waterproof containers and late at night lowered silently through a porthole on the offshore side in a pre-arranged area. Later, also at night, the pickup crew employed by the syndicate would have little trouble locating the containers on the bottom with their especially-built drag. The pickup crew would wait, of course, until no ship occupied the berth, and therefore the vicinity ordinarily would be clear of Customs officers.

The paneling method of smuggling was so successful that syndicate shippers of contraband were known to pay the shoreside Chinese hiring agent immense sums to place their particular crew on these vessels.

Finally, competition between shipping groups became so fierce that we were furnished gratis detailed information by one syndicate against another. This enabled us to break up all the rackets of this kind.

Shortly thereafter, the American seafaring unions brought enough pressure to bear on both the government and the steamship operators to require the American President Line and all other American flag ships to employ only American crew members.

This dealt a killing blow to several of the smuggling syndicates.

Suicide Preferred

A BEAUTIFUL EURASIAN GIRL named Molly Maria Wendt arrived at San Pedro, California as a passenger on a Japanese vessel from Shanghai, China. It was summer, 1936.

When searched, her numerous pieces of baggage yielded fifty-four pounds of heroin.

Upon questioning by Los Angeles Customs officers, she told them she had been instructed to deliver the heroin to a "man in black" at a certain hotel on a certain date. Customs placed her in the hotel to await the transaction.

A woman clerk from the Customs office was assigned to guard Molly, and two Customs officers were stationed in an adjoining room.

That night, Miss Wendt decided to take a shower. Since the bathroom had only one door which opened into the hotel room, and a small, high window, the woman guard saw no reason why Molly shouldn't bathe in privacy.

After ten minutes or so of listening to a musical program on the radio, which partly dulled the sound of the water spraying from the shower, the custodian began to wonder why Molly was taking so much time.

Knocking on the door repeatedly, she waited for an answer. None came. Then she tried the knob and found that Molly had noiselessly locked it.

Alarmed, she quickly summoned the agents in the adjoining room by the pre-arranged signal of pounding on the wall.

The officers hurriedly rushed in and broke open the bathroom door with several hard kicks.

The small, steamy bathroom was empty.

"Where on earth—she couldn't get out of here," cried the clerk, frantically pushing back the shower curtain to shut off the water.

"She couldn't, but she did," answered one of the agents.

Molly's expensive Oriental silk pajamas and robe were gone, too.

The other agent examined the small window above his head.

"If she crawled through here she didn't even break the glass," he guessed. "Maybe she's a female Houdini!"

The hunt began for what turned out to be an elusive young woman. Officers all over the country searched planes, trains, and buses. Several Eurasian girls were found, but none was Molly Wendt.

A few days afterward, a watchful Customs Inspector in New York saw a woman answering Molly's description going aboard a Hamburg-American liner. He took his suspect to the office of the Supervising Customs Agent in New York. This officer was known by all Customs Agents as being a tough, hard-working, sincere officer who would believe nothing without satisfactory proof.

He had the Eurasian girl fingerprinted, then questioned her in detail. She denied vehemently that she was Molly Maria Wendt. She said her ship was sailing in a short time and if she were forced to miss it she would initiate action against all those responsible for her treatment.

The girl finally convinced the Supervising Agent that she was not the now much-sought Molly Wendt. Taken back to her ship by the Inspector, she got aboard shortly before it was due to leave for Europe.

As soon as she left his office, the Supervising Agent wired the girl's fingerprint description to our Los Angeles office. He was stunned to learn they were Molly's, the girl who had been in his office a short time ago.

This was a severe shock to this particular Supervising Agent who had a thirty-year record as a top law enforcement man. He had listened to hundreds of smugglers, important and unimportant, over the years. He had attained a reputation as one of the best cross-examiners of suspects in the entire Agency Service, and not one who was readily fooled.

The sudden impact, as he realized that he had let the much-sought Molly Maria Wendt leave his office, was calamitous. He recalled also that Treasury Secretary Morgenthau himself had become interested in this particular case and had advised all Customs ports of exit to be on the watch for Molly.

The Supervising Agent hurriedly telephoned the Customs officer who was in charge of the pier where the vessel was berthed. He was told that, due to a pilot delay, the ship was still at the pier, but the pilot was now aboard and the vessel was expected to sail momentarily.

"Hold that ship, by all means until my agent gets there," directed the agitated Supervisor.

Rushing aboard the ship, the Customs officer ordered the pilot and the Captain to remain at the pier. An agent from the Supervising Agent's office arrived, which actually took just a few minutes, since he was only several blocks away. He took Molly in custody and back to confront the man she had fooled with her cool demeanor and apparent innocence.

The Eurasian girl then admitted her true identity. She was transferred at once to Los Angeles.

There she was questioned at great length. Customs officers learned that this was her trial run and that she was on her way to Mexico City with the heroin. She was to deliver it to a man named Brandstatter, who was the head of the Machinery and Engineering Corporation of Shanghai, China. She named others as well whose headquarters were in Mexico City, among them Maurico Eghise, a son-in-law of the Chief of Police of Mexico City.

A few days after the newspapers had headlined the word of Molly's arrest in New York, the body of a German doctor, a close friend of Molly's in Shanghai, was found with his throat cut. There was considerable speculation among the agents familiar with Molly's case as to whether it was a case of suicide, or whether the narcotics gang had murdered him, believing he had informed on the girl.

While holding Molly in Los Angeles for trial, U.S. Agents began an investigation in Mexico City concerning the persons mentioned by Molly as being involved in the smuggling plot.

Soon after the inquiry began, Maurico Eghise, son-in-law of Mexico City's Police Chief, attempted to commit suicide by slashing his throat. However, he missed his jugular vein, recovered, and was deported to his native Turkey.

Shortly after our agents went to Mexico City, Brandstatter, named by Molly as the head of the smuggling syndicate, left for Havana, Cuba.

In Havana he booked passage on the SS *Oriente* for Spain. Our men learned of Brandstatter's departure and, through representatives of the steamship line, were able to have the *Oriente* routed to Spain via New York.

On the morning the *Oriente* entered New York harbor, Brandstatter went on deck. When, to his amazement, he saw where he was, he realized the game was up for him. He returned to his stateroom and hanged himself with the sash from his bathrobe.

Molly pleaded guilty at her trial and was sentenced to the Federal prison at Alderson, West Virginia, for ten years. After serving a short time, she was found to have an advanced case of tuberculosis, and was allowed to return to China.

The official file in this case in the Customs Bureau is probably entitled *U.S. vs Wendt et al.*, but to many Customs Agents it is known as the case of "Suicide Preferred."

Recollections

AFTER THE CLOSE OF THE FIRST World War, I received my honorable discharge from the United States Navy as a Chief Petty Officer in November, 1919.

At my home in Portland, Oregon, I took a civil service examination and on June 1, 1920, entered the U.S. Customs Service as an Inspector of Customs. I was twenty-five years old.

The Customs Service consists of many divisions and duties. I wanted assignment with the law enforcement section. In a port the size of Portland, there was no regularly established Customs Agent's office at that time.

The Customs Agency Service, which operates under a Deputy Commissioner in Washington, D. C., is the detective division of the Service. Their personnel are chosen from the ranks of the general Customs Service. Inspectors, however, have law enforcement responsibility. One must serve an apprenticeship before getting into the Agency Service. I was quite happy to get the opportunity to begin as an Inspector in my home town. My assignment was first to the "searching squad" under the immediate supervision of a twenty-year veteran of the Service, Inspector W. B. Crewdson.

Among ships of many nationalities calling in the Columbia and Willamette rivers at that time, there was a great number of Japanese freighters engaged in carrying logs and lumber to Japan. It was not unusual to see forty vessels of this flag in the Columbia river at the same time.

These ships were scattered at lumber mills and log loading booms all along the 105 miles between Portland and Astoria at the mouth of the Columbia—an ideal setup for smuggling.

There was a huge demand for Japanese beads, Russian vodka and Oriental silk garments. There was an even greater demand for liquor from any country, as the Eighteenth Amendment was then in effect.

Inspector Crewdson, my boss, was the most patient and thorough of Customs officers. He took his job so seriously that he probably dreamed every night of smugglers, planning some new way to outwit them. As for the smugglers, they must have had sleepless nights also.

One of our routine jobs and one that caused us many headaches was to search every incoming ship for contraband. That may sound simple enough, but searching a ship is like ransacking a city.

Remember that a ship has refrigeration, oil and water storage tanks, passenger cabins, some with paneling, storage rooms, ventilator shafts, hundreds of lockers, and other hiding places. Each of these affords ample opportunity for concealing contraband.

Imagine trying to find the merchandise the smugglers have spent so much time and thought in hiding away. And remember that an opium can is about the size and shape of a half-pound tobacco can, and that a fortune in pearls can be hidden inside a loaf of bread.

For instance, you go down into the engine room to

search. You are in a maze of pipes and other strange pieces of equipment. Which of these are legitimate and which are there solely to conceal contraband?

Then go into the cabins. Have you a blueprint of the vessel so you can tell whether those are false walls? Or which of those similar compartments contains a washstand and which a cache of silk lingerie?

Crewdson taught us to be suspicious of any part of a ship which had been newly painted. On one occasion we noticed that the manhole plates covering an oil tank were glistening with fresh paint. We promptly removed the plates. I stripped and went into the tank, carrying a long rod.

I poked and probed and all but suffocated from the fumes. But my discomfort paid off, for I located a package anchored to the bottom. When we fished this out and opened it, we were in possession of hundreds of strings of beads and fifty pint cans of vodka.

Another time, searching a ship having a Chinese crew, we noticed they remained quite calm and indifferent to our efforts—until we reached a large ventilator. Then the entire group started jabbering to one another, in Chinese, of course. They talked so loud we could hardly think. (Which, perhaps, was their object.)

We tied a rope around the waist of the smallest member of our party and lowered him down the ventilator. At the first turn, he discovered fifty cans of opium.

Thoroughly suspicious now, Crewdson demanded the blueprints of the ship. With them we discovered that a large pipe in the engine room was not on the prints. The "black gang" swore it was part of the ventilator system and had just been installed. But we went to work on it. And we struck pay dirt. In that innocent-looking pipe were more than a thousand cans of opium selling at the time for about forty American dollars a can.

These are samples of what we were up against.

Once we searched the bosun's locker on a ship arriving from Hong Kong. Inside we found four hundred cans of hop (opium) wrapped in canvas packages and each tied with a peculiar type of rope.

Of course we accused the bosun, a Chinese, but he denied his guilt vehemently. We showed him one of the packages and he declared that the rope was the same kind as that owned by two of his crew.

We had taken him ashore to the office for questioning. On his promise to deliver the two guilty crewmen, we returned with him to the ship at midnight. The vessel apparently was deserted except for the watchman peacefully sleeping near the gangplank. As soon as we reached the deck the bosun blew his pipe and gave a loud screech in Chinese. Instantly, forty or fifty Chinese seamen appeared, apparently out of thin air. The bosun harangued them in their native tongue, and they jabbered back at him.

This went on for some time, then two of the group stepped forward and sullenly admitted their guilt. We put them in jail, and that was that. But I've always wondered whether the bosun had passed the buck and made them the scapegoats.

Being a very thorough man, Crewdson had learned plenty of the smugglers' tricks through the years. One of their pet stunts was to telephone us anonymously, informing us that a ship was "hot" and advising us in detail just how to find the contraband she carried.

The object, of course, was to call our attention to a vessel miles away from the one which carried the caller's own contraband. While we were searching it, he would have a clear route for getting his own stuff to safety.

Crewdson had fallen for this ruse only once or twice before he caught on. So when one of these messages came in, he would split us into groups which covered both ends of the harbor at once. Generally, this gave us a double haul.

Dave Lightner, one of these clever "search-the-other-ship" planners, had his ruse boomerang right back into his face. He was skilled at finding out his competitors' operations and tipping us off to them. We actually made several important seizures on his tips. But then when we began playing both ends against the middle, we got him—along with about five thousand ounces of opium.

It was hard work with long hours, but I never lost interest in it.

Prohibition had now come of age and the first, faltering attempts to smuggle in liquor from Canada had become a well-organized business. Large cargoes began coming in by truck and car, cargoes it was our job to discover and confiscate.

There were only four possible crossings of the Columbia River for the rum runners. Three were across ferries and the fourth by the toll bridge at Vancouver, Washington. We would cover each of these in turn since our lack of personnel prevented guarding all simultaneously. Whenever we saw a heavily loaded auto or truck approaching the crossing we were watching, we would stop it and search. This got results for a time, then the smugglers pulled a new stunt.

The runners began loading trucks so heavily with scrap iron, discarded boilers and similar junk that the springs sagged. They would use these as pilot vehicles and send them across a ferry or the toll bridge. If this decoy didn't bring us out of hiding, they felt the way was clear and gave the signal for the real smuggler to run the gantlet.

For many frigid nights I hid in the lavatory of the toll collector's office on the bridge, watching for liquor-laden vehicles.

We soon got wise to the pilot car trick and learned to let it bump past unchallenged. Often we'd see it return to the other bank and pass the word that the road was clear. On the next try the rum runners would find they were wrong.

In December, 1925, I was promoted to Customs Agent. When the Collector of Customs at Portland called me in to show me a wire just received from the Commissioner of Customs in Washington, D.C., advising of my promotion to Customs Agent, one of my highest ambitions was realized.

To say that I was pleased is a major understatement. Customs Agents were assigned all over the world, did much traveling, and always had some difficult or unusual smuggling case to solve.

I was directed to report to the Supervising Customs Agent in New York immediately for temporary duty.

My instructions were to go to Supervising Agent Wheatley's home after office hours. It was specified I was not to go to his office. He lived in an apartment in Brooklyn.

Upon reporting to Mr. Wheatley, he told me I was to work with two Agents from Florida, Edson J. Shamhart and Bill Harmon, on a personnel case involving some Customs officers. We had been chosen because we were unknown in that area.

He turned the three of us over to Customs Agent Elmer J. Lewis, under whose immediate direction we were to operate. Lewis later became Supervising Agent at New York. Ed Shamhart eventually became Deputy Commissioner of Customs in Washington, in charge of all Customs Agents, and Bill Harmon rose to Supervising Agent at El Paso, Texas. So I was working with some topnotchers.

In about two months we were able to prove the guilt of some of the officers, as well as the innocence of others whom we were investigating.

During this investigation I had a rather amusing experience. While in the Navy, I had been a shipmate on the cruiser *Galveston* with a Chief Gunner's Mate known familiarly by the nickname of "Chow". The *Galveston* served on convoy duty for a time during World War I and we had been in and out of New York several times. Now, whom should I meet on Broadway but my old friend of six years earlier, Chow, himself!

Chow recognized me immediately and seemed as glad to see me as I was to meet him again after some years.

He told me he had been retired after thirty years of Naval service. He now had a job as Chief Engineer of a rum vessel out on "Rum Row". He insisted that he had enough influence with the rummies to get me a good job with the rum fleet, too!

"This job pays good money, and you don't have to work too much," Chow urged.

I had a hard time convincing him that I didn't want such a job without revealing that I was a Federal law enforcement officer. When we parted I had the feeling that Chow was quite disgusted with me for not taking advantage of what seemed to him a wonderful opportunity to better myself.

After the New York case was completed, I received temporary duty in San Francisco, working on a liquor smuggling conspiracy case to be presented to the U.S. attorney. The case involved rum running activities on the part of a group known as the Swede Gang.

It was while on this assignment that I met the young prosecuting attorney for Alameda County, California. His investigators were checking certain officials suspected of possible connections with the rum runners. This youthful prosecutor was full of vim and go and attained maximum success in his cases. He originally was a farm boy from the vicinity of Bakersfield, California. His name was Earl Warren, who was destined to become Chief Justice of the U.S. Supreme Court.

During the same period that we were investigating the Swede Gang, we were also looking into the rum running activities of an Italian known as Tony Cornero. Many years later, Tony ran into trouble with the state of California and

Attorney General Earl Warren when he tried to operate a gambling ship that was anchored in Santa Monica bight.

The ship was anchored more than three miles from the shore line at any one point, but was less than three miles from an imaginary line drawn from outer shore to outer shore of the bight. Mr. Warren won his argument on this matter in the state courts. As a result, the gambling ship was seized and put out of business.

Tony Cornero, whose real name was Anthony Scalla, was indicted by the Federal Grand Jury at San Francisco on our rum running investigation. He made a getaway to Canada, though, with his red-haired girl friend before the warrant of arrest could be served on him.

One of our Seattle agents met the train on which Tony and his paramour were fleeing when it reached the outskirts of Portland. Tony must have been warned, because when the agent reached the dining car where the train conductor had told him Tony could be found, the Italian's seat was vacant. His girl friend was there, and food was on the table, but the window was wide open.

Evidently Tony had climbed out the window while the train was moving slowly through town. We all decided that Tony's most important feat was getting the dining car window open. None of us had ever been able to accomplish that trick.

It wasn't long, however, before Tony decided to return and stand trial on the liquor smuggling conspiracy in San Francisco.

Soon after returning to the Pacific coast, I began to specialize in narcotic smuggling violations, which have been described in this book.

When World War II came along, I was commissioned a Lieutenant Commander in the Coast Guard and assigned to Eleventh District Coast Guard headquarters at Long Beach,

California. I served as the District Intelligence Officer under Captain—later Rear Admiral—William Towle.

Our Intelligence unit soon grew to two hundred enlisted men, thirty-eight women Spars and seven commissioned officers. Our duty was to screen all persons employed near the waterfront and to try to insure the safety of the Los Angeles —Long Beach harbors. With important shipyards and highly volatile oil and gas supplies, the utmost vigilance was imperative.

During the four-year war period, we brought about the removal from the waterfront of an average of thirty persons as month. These persons included suspected spies and saboteurs as well as others who might possibly be dangerous to waterfront installations. For instance, on one occasion we found an escapee from a hospital for the criminally insane working on an oil tanker loading highly explosive fuel. He had a record of setting fires. If you multiply these instances by a thousand or two, you can see our problems during the war years.

On March 1, 1949, I retired from the Customs Service, and on March 1, 1955, I retired from the Coast Guard with the rank of Captain.